AFTER THE RESURRECTION

AFTER THE RESURRECTION

Including a Study Guide for
Private Meditation and Public Discussion

Alexander MacLaren

KREGEL PUBLICATIONS
Grand Rapids, Michigan 49501

After the Resurrection by Alexander Maclaren. © 1992 by Kregel Publications. All rights reserved. This book was originally published by Hodder and Stoughton in London, England, in 1902. It was later printed by Klock and Klock in a 1985 reprint edition combined with *The Appearances of Our Lord After the Passion* by Henry Barclay Swete in a book called *The Post-Resurrection Ministry of Christ.* The first chapter, "The Grave of the Dead John and the Grave of the Living Christ" is taken from Maclaren's *The Secret of Power* (Funk & Wagnalls, New York, 1902). It is included because it introduces the post-Resurrection appearances of Jesus in a very graphic and gripping way.

Scripture text used in this book is the Authorized King James Version. Those marked NIV are from the Holy Bible, New International Version, © 1978 by the International Bible Society.

Cover photo: Art Jacobs
Cover & book design: Al Hartman

Library of Congress Cataloging-in-Publication Data
MacLaren, Alexander, 1826-1910.
After the Resurrection / Alexander MacLaren.
     p.   cm.
1. Jesus Christ—Appearances. 2. Jesus Christ— Forty days. I. Title.
BT490.M33   1992   232.9'7—dc20   91-21642
                                                        CIP

ISBN 0-8254-3199-9

1 2 3 4 5 Printing/Year 96 95 94 93 92

Printed in the United States of America

Contents

Foreword

I first learned of "The Invisible College" about twenty years ago from Dr. Howard Hendricks of Dallas Theological Seminary. He exhorted those of us in his class to "enroll" in this college upon graduation. It was, he said, the only way our seminary studies could be given depth as well as breadth and retain relevance in the present while also drawing needed inspiration from the past. Since then, articles have been written in different journals extolling the virtues of "The Invisible College," for as Thomas Carlyle said in *Heroes and Hero-Worship*, "The true university of these days is a collection of books," and it is from our colleagues and friends that we learn about those books that are worth acquiring and reading.

Often neglected in today's theological milieu is the post-resurrection ministry of Christ. Justifiable emphasis is made upon His virgin conception, sinless life, atoning death and bodily resurrection. Few writers, however, have probed His ministry during the 40 days before His ascension.

This book by Alexander MacLaren traces the events of Christ's resurrection (the first chapter deals with the impact of a belief in the resurrection upon the early disciples) and the biblical evidence of

Christ's bodily resurrection and ministry, rescuing the subject from the trammels of negative biblical criticism which has flourished in recent years.

Born in Scotland, MacLaren received his early training at Stepney College (affiliated with London University) and graduated with his bachelor's degree in 1845. His first pastoral charge was in South Hampton where he built a remarkably strong group of believers. In 1858 he was called to Manchester and remained there for the rest of his life. On numerous occasions, he preached for the Baptist Missionary Society, the London Missionary Society and also served as president of the Baptist World Congress. The universities of Edinburgh, Manchester and Glasgow each honored him with doctorates. His most enduring legacy is his *Expositions of Holy Scripture*, which has been reprinted on numerous occasions in a variety of formats. Dr. MacLaren also supplied important commentaries on the book of Psalms and the Epistles to the Colossians and Philemon in *The Expositor's Bible*.

MacLaren was a prolific writer. His treatment of the post-resurrection appearances of Christ received acclaim in secular as well as religious journals. Here are a few excerpts taken from periodicals of that time:

[The] work of a brilliant and effective teacher. Dr. MacLaren writes with real power and insight.   —*Saturday Review*

Dr. MacLaren has evidently mastered his subject with the aid of the best authorities, and has put the results of his studies before his readers in a most attractive form. . . . It is written in a charming style [and] we only give to it the praise which is its due.

—*Scotsman*

CYRIL J. BARBER
Author, *The Minister's Library*

The grave of John was the end of a "school." The grave of Jesus was the beginning of the church. Why? The only answer is the message which the women brought back from the empty sepulcher on that Easter day: "The Lord is risen." The whole history of the Christian church, and even its very existence, is unintelligible, except on the supposition of the resurrection. But for that, the fate of John's disciples would have been the fate of Christ's—they would have melted away into the mass of the nation, and at most there would have been one more petty Galilean sect, that would have lived on for a generation and died out when the last of His companions died.

1

The Grave of the Dead John and the Grave of the Living Jesus

And John's disciples came, and took up the body, and buried it, and went and told Jesus. —Matthew 14:12

And they departed quickly from the sepulcher with fear and great joy. —Matthew 28:8

There is a remarkable parallel and still more remarkable contrast between these two groups of disciples at the graves of their respective masters. John the Baptist's followers ventured into the very jaws of the lion to rescue the headless corpse of their martyred teacher from a prison grave. They bore it away and lay it reverently in its unknown sepulcher, and when they had done these last offices of love they felt that all was over. They no longer had a center, and they disintegrated. There was nothing to hold them together any more. The shepherd had been smitten, and the flock were scattered. As a "school" or a distinct community they ceased to be, and were mostly absorbed into the ranks of Christ's followers. That sorrowful little company who turned from John's grave, perhaps amidst the grim rocks of Moab, perhaps in his native city amongst the hills of Judah, parted, then, to meet no more, and to bear away only a common sorrow that time would comfort, and a common memory that time would dim.

The other group laid their martyred Master in His grave with as tender hands and as little hope as did John's disciples. The bond that held them together was gone too, and the disintegrating process began at once. We see them breaking up into little knots, and soon they, too, will be scattered. The women come to the grave to perform the woman's office of anointing, and they are left to go alone. Other slight hints are given which show how much the ties of companionship had been relaxed, even in a day, and how certainly and quickly they would have fallen asunder. But all at once a new element comes in, all is changed. The earliest visitors to the sepulcher leave it, not with the lingering sorrow of those who have no more that they can do, but with the quick buoyant step of people charged with great and glad tidings. They come to it wrapped in grief—they leave it with great joy. They come to it, feeling that all was over, and their union with the rest who had loved Him was little more than a remembrance. They go away feeling that they are bound together more closely than ever.

The grave of John was the end of a "school." The grave of Jesus was the beginning of the church. Why? The only answer is the message which the women brought back from the empty sepulcher on that Easter day: "The Lord is risen." The whole history of the Christian church, and even its very existence, is unintelligible, except on the supposition of the resurrection. But for that, the fate of John's disciples would have been the fate of Christ's—they would have melted away into the mass of the nation, and at most there would have been one more petty Galilean sect, that would have lived on for a generation and died out when the last of His companions died.

So from these two contrasted groups we may fairly gather some thoughts as to the resurrection of Christ, as attested by the very existence of a Christian church, and as to the joy of that resurrection.

THE RESURRECTION
UNITED THE DISCIPLES

Now the first point to be considered is that the conduct of Christ's disciples after His death was exactly the opposite of what might have been expected.

They held together. The natural thing for them to do would have been to disband as did the followers of John the Baptist; for the one bond was gone; and if they had acted according to the ordinary laws of human conduct they would have said to them-selves, "Let us go back to our fishing-boats and our tax-gathering, and seek safety in separation, and nurse our sorrow apart." A few lingering days might have been given to weep together at His grave, and to assuage the first bitterness of grief and disappoint-ment; but when these were over, nothing could have prevented Christianity and the church from being buried in the same sep-ulcher as Jesus. As certainly as the stopping up of the fountain would empty the river's bed, so surely would Christ's death have scattered His disciples. And that strange fact, that it did not scatter them, needs to be examined carefully and fairly account-ed for in some plausible manner. The end of John's school gives a parallel which brings the singularity of the fact into the stron-ger relief. Looking at these two groups as they stand before us in these two texts, the question is irresistibly suggested, Why did not the one fall away into its separate elements, as the other did? The keystone of the arch was in both cases withdrawn—why did the one structure topple into ruin while the other stood firm?

Not only did the disciples of Christ keep united, but their conceptions of Jesus underwent a remarkable change, on His death. We might have expected indeed that, when memory began to work, and the disturbing influence of daily association was withdrawn, the same idealizing process would have begun on their image of Him, which reveals and ennobles the characters of our dear ones who have gone away from us. Most men have to die before their true beauty is discerned. But no process of that sort will suffice to account for the change and heightening of the disciples' thoughts about their dead Lord. It was not merely that, as the disciples on the way to Emmaus remembered, they said, "Did not our hearts burn within us by the way while He talked with us?"—but that His death wrought exactly the opposite effect from what it might have been expected to do.

It ought to have ended their hope that He was the Messiah, and we know that within forty-eight hours it was beginning to do so, as we learn from the plaintive words of disappointed and fading hope: "We trusted that it had been He which should have redeemed Israel." If, so early, the cold conviction was stealing over their hearts that their dearest expectation was proved by His death to have been a dream, what could have prevented its entire dominion over them, as the days grew into months and years?

But somehow or other that process was arrested, and the opposite one set in. The death that should have shattered Messianic dreams confirmed them. The death that should have cast a deeper shadow of incomprehensibleness over His strange and lofty claims poured a new light upon them, which made them all plain and clear. The very parts of His teaching which His death would have made those who loved Him wish to forget, became the center of His followers' faith. His cross became His throne. While He lived with them they knew not what He said in His deepest words, but, by a strange paradox, His death convinced them that He was the Son of God, and that what they had seen with their eyes, and their hands had handled, was the eternal life. The cross alone could never have done that. Something else there must have been, if the men were sane, to account for this paradox.

Nor is this all. Another equally unlikely sequel of the death of

Jesus is the unmistakable moral transformation effected on the disciples. Timorous and tremulous before, something or other touched them into altogether new boldness and self-possession. Dependent on His presence before, and helpless when He was away from them for an hour, they become all at once strong and calm; they stand before the fury of a Jewish mob and the threatenings of the Sanhedrin, unmoved and victorious. And these brave confessors and saintly heroes are the men who, a few weeks before, had been petulant, self-willed, jealous, cowardly. What had lifted them suddenly so far above themselves? Their Master's death? That would more naturally have taken any heart of courage out of them, and left them indeed as sheep in the midst of wolves. Why, then, do they thus strangely blaze up into grandeur and heroism? Can any reasonable account be given of these paradoxes? Surely it is not too much to ask of people who profess to explain Christianity on naturalistic principles, that they shall make the process clear to us by which, Christ being dead and buried, His disciples were kept together, learned to think more loftily of Him and sprang at once to a new grandeur of character. Why did they not do as John's disciples did, and disappear? Why was not the stream lost in the sand, when the head-waters were cut off?

THE RESURRECTION ATTESTED
BY THE CHURCH

Notice then, next, that the disciples' immediate belief in the Resurrection furnishes a reasonable, and the only reasonable, explanation of the facts. There is no better historical evidence of a fact than the existence of an institution built upon it, and coeval with it. The Christian church is such evidence for the fact of the Resurrection; or, to put the conclusion in the most moderate fashion, for the belief in the Resurrection. For, as we have shown, the natural effect of our Lord's death would have been to shatter the whole fabric: and if that effect were not produced, the only reasonable account of the force that hindered it is, that His followers believed that He rose again. Since that was their faith, one can understand how they were banded more closely together than ever. One can understand how their eyes were opened to know Him who was "declared to be the Son of God with power by the resurrection from the dead" (Rom. 1:4). One can understand how, in the enthusiasm of these new thoughts of their Lord, and in the strength of His victory over death, they put aside their old fears and littlenesses and clothed themselves in armor of light. "The Lord is risen indeed" was the belief which made the continuous existence of the church possible. Any other explanation of that great outstanding fact is lame and hopelessly insufficient.

We know that this belief was the belief of the early church. Even if one waived all reference to the gospels we have the means of demonstrating that in Paul's undisputed epistles. Nobody has questioned that he wrote the First Epistle to the Corinthians. The date most generally assumed to that letter brings it within about twenty-five years of the crucifixion. In that letter, in addition to a multitude of incidental references to the Lord as risen, we have the great passage in the fifteenth chapter, where the apostle not only declares that the Resurrection was one of the two facts which made his "gospel," but solemnly enumerates the witnesses of the risen Lord, and alleges that this gospel of the resurrection was common to him and to all the church. He tells us of Christ's appearance to himself at his conversion, which must have taken place within six or seven years of the crucifixion, and assures us that at that early period he found the whole church believing and preaching Christ's resurrection. Their belief rested on their alleged meeting with Him a few days after His death, and it is inconceivable that within so short a period such a belief should have sprung up and been universally received if it had not begun when and as they said it did.

But we are not left even to inferences of this kind to show that from the beginning the church witnessed to the resurrection of Jesus. Its own existence is the great witness to its faith.

And it is important to observe that, even if we had not the documentary evidence of the Pauline epistles as the earliest records of the gospels, and of the Acts of the Apostles, we should still have sufficient proof that the belief in the Resurrection is as old as the church. For the continuance of the church cannot be explained without it. If that faith had not dawned on their slow, sad hearts on that Easter morning, a few weeks would have seen them scattered: and if once they had been scattered, as they inevitably would have been, no power could have reunited them, any more than a diamond once shattered can be pieced together again. There would have been no motive and no actors to frame a story of resurrection when once the little company had melted away. The existence of the church depended on their belief that the Lord was risen. In the nature of the case that belief must have followed immediately on His death. It, and it only, reasonably accounts for the facts. And so, over and above apostles, and gospels, and epistles, the church is the great witness, by its very being, to its own immediate and continuous belief in the resurrection of our Lord.

THE RESURRECTION WAS A FACT

Again, we may remark that such a belief could not have originated or maintained itself unless it had been true.

Our previous remarks have gone no farther than to establish the belief in the resurrection of Christ, as the basis of primitive Christianity. It is vehemently alleged, and we may freely admit, that the step is a long one from subjective belief to objective reality. But still it is surely perfectly fair to argue that a given belief is of such a nature that it cannot be supposed to rest on anything less solid than a fact; and this is eminently the case in regard to the belief in Christ's resurrection. There have been many attempts on the part of those who reject that belief to account for its existence, and each of them in succession has "had its day, and ceased to be." Unbelief devours its own children remorselessly, and the succession to the throne of anti-Christian skepticism is won, as in some barbarous tribes, by slaying the reigning sovereign. The armies of the aliens turn their weapons against one another, and each new assailant of the historical veracity of the gospels commences operations by showing that all previous assailants have been wrong, and that none of their explanations will hold water.

For instance, we hear nothing now of the coarse old explanation that the story of the Resurrection was a lie, and became current through the conscious imposture of the leaders of the church. And it was high time that such a solution should be laid aside. Who, with half an eye for character, could study the deeds and writings of the apostles, and not feel that, whatever else they were, they were profoundly honest, and as convinced as of their own existence, that they had seen Christ "alive after His passion, by many infallible proofs"? If Paul and Peter and John were conspirators in a trick, then their lives and their words were the most astounding anomaly. Who, either, that had the faintest perception of the forces that sway opinion and frame systems, could believe that the fair fabric of Christian morality was built bubbling up from the very pit of hell? Do men gather grapes of thorns, or figs of thistles? That insolent hypothesis has had its day.

Then when it was discredited, we were told the mythical tendency would explain everything. It showed us how good men could tell lies without knowing it, and how the religious value of an alleged fact in an alleged historical revelation did not in the least depend on its being a fact. And that great discovery, which first converted solid historical Christianity into a gaseous condition, and then caught the fumes in some kind of retort, and professed to hand us them back again improved by the sublimation, has pretty well gone the way of all hypotheses. Myths are not made in three days, or in three years, and no more tie can be allowed for the formation of the myth of the Resurrection. What was the church to feed on while the myth was growing? It would have been starved to death long before.

Then, the last new explanation which is gravely put forward, and is the prevailing one now, sustains itself by reference to undeniable facts in the history of religious movements, and of such abnormal attitudes of the mind as modern spiritualism. On the strength of which analogy we are invited to see in the faith of the early Christians in the resurrection of the Lord a gigantic instance of "hallucination." No doubt there have been, and still are, extraordinary instances of its power, especially in minds excited by religious ideas. But we have only to consider the details of the facts in hand to feel that they cannot be accounted for on such a ground.

Do hallucinations lay hold on five hundred people at once? Does a hallucination last for a long country walk, and give rise to protracted conversation? Does hallucination explain the story of Christ eating and drinking before His disciples? The uncertain twilight of the garden might have begotten such an airy phantom in the brain of a single sobbing woman; but the appearances to be explained are so numerous, so varied in character, embrace so many details, appeal to so many of the senses—the ear and hand as well as to the eye —were spread over so long a period, and were simultaneously shared by so large a number, that no theory of such a sort can account for them, unless by impugning the veracity of the records. And then we are back again on the old abandoned ground of deceit and imposture. It sounds plausible to say, "Hallucination is a proved cause of many a supposed supernatural event—why not of this?" But the plausibility of the solution ceases as soon as you try it on the actual facts in their variety and completeness. It has to be eked out with a length of the fox's skin of deceit before it covers them; and we may confidently assert that such a belief as the belief of the early church in the resurrection of the Lord was never the product either of deceit or of illusion, or of any amalgam of the two.

What new solutions the fertility of unbelief may yet bring forth, and the credulity of unbelief may yet accept, we know not: but we may firmly hold by the faith which breathed new hope and strange joy into that sad band on the first Easter morning, and rejoice with them in the glad wonderful fact that Christ is risen from the dead.

THE JOY OF THE RESURRECTION

For the message of the Resurrection is a message to us as truly as to the heavy-hearted unbelieving men that first received it. We may think for a moment of the joy with which *we* should return from the sepulcher of the risen Savior.

How little these women knew that, as they went back from the grave in the morning twilight, they were the bearers of "great joy which should be to all people!" To them and to the first hearers of their message there would be little clear in the rush of glad surprise, beyond the blessed thought, *then He is not gone from us altogether.* Sweet visions of the resumption of happy companionship would fill their minds, and it would not be until calmer moments that the stupendous significance of the fact would reveal itself.

Mary's rapturous gesture to clasp Christ by the feet, when the certainty that it was in very deed He, flooded her soul with dazzling light, reveals her first emotion, which no doubt was also the first with them all, "Then we shall have Him with us again, and all the old joy of companionship will be ours once more." Nor were they wrong in thinking so, however little they as yet understood the future manner of their fellowship, or anticipated His leaving them so soon. Nor are we without a share even in that phase of their joy; for the resurrection of Jesus Christ gives us a living Lord for our love, an ever present Companion and Brother for our hearts to hold, even if our hands cannot clasp Him by the feet. A dead Christ might have been the object of faint historical admiration, and the fair statue might have stood amidst others in the halls of the world; but the risen, living Christ can love and be loved, and we too may be glad with the joy of those who have found a heart to rest their hearts upon, and a companionship that can never fail.

As the early disciples learned to reflect upon the fact of Christ's resurrection, its riches unfolded themselves by degrees, and the earliest aspect of its "power" was the light it shed on His person and work. Taught by it, as we have seen, they recognized Him for the Messiah whom they had long expected, and for something more—the Incarnate Son of God.

That phase of their joy belongs to us too. If Christ, who made such avowals of His nature as we know He did, and hazarded such assertions of His claims, His personality and His office, as fill the gospels, were really laid in the grave and saw corruption, then the assertions are disproved, the claims unwarranted, the office a figment of His imagination. He may still remain a great teacher, with a tremendous deduction to be made from the worth of His teaching. But all that is deepest in His own words about Himself, and His relation to men, must be sorrowfully put on one side. But if He, after such assertions and claims, rose from the dead, and rising, dieth no more, then for the last time, and in the mightiest tones, the voice that rent the heavens at His baptism and His transfiguration proclaims: "This is My beloved Son; hear ye Him" (Mark 9:11). Our joy in His resurrection is the joy of those to whom He is therein declared to be the Son of God, and who see in Christ risen their accepted Sacrifice, and their ever-living Redeemer.

Such was the earliest effect of the resurrection of Jesus, if we trust the records of apostolic preaching. Then by degrees the joyful thought took shape in the church's consciousness that their Shepherd had gone before them into the dark pen where death pastured his flocks, and had taken it for His own, for the quiet resting-place where He would make them lie down by still waters, and whence He would lead them out to the lofty mountains where His fold should be. The power of Christ's resurrection as the pattern and pledge of ours is the final source of the joy which may fill our hearts as we turn away from that empty sepulcher.

The world has guessed and feared, or guessed and hoped, but always guessed and doubted the life beyond. Analogies, poetic adumbrations, probabilities drawn from consciousness and from conscience, from intuition and from anticipation, are but poor foundations on which to build a solid faith. But to those to whom the resurrection of Christ is a fact their own future life is a fact. Here we have a solid certainty, and here alone. The heart says as we lay our dear ones in the grave, "Surely we part not for ever." The conscience says, as it points us to our own evil deeds, "After death the judgment." A deep indestructible instinct prophesies in every breast of a future. But all is vague and doubtful.

The one proof of a life beyond the grave is the resurrection of Jesus Christ. Therefore, let us be glad with the gladness of men plucked from a dark abyss of doubt and uncertainty, and planted on the rock of solid certainty; and let us rejoice with joy unspeakable, and laden with a prophetic weight of glory, as we ring out the ancient Easter morning's greeting, "The Lord is risen indeed!" (Luke 24:34).

What was the touch that was forbidden? On that very morning other women were permitted to clasp His feet. On that very evening He said to the apostles, in effect, "Handle Me and see." A week after He said to the doubter, "Reach hither thy hand. Thrust it into My side" (John 20:27). Why were they permitted what was forbidden to Mary? For this simple reason, that her attempt to clasp Him was the expression of a love and a faith which unduly clung to the external form, and which desired to perpetuate the vanished relationship. And so our Lord began the educational process, then and there.

2

Touch Me Not

*Jesus saith unto her, Touch Me not; for I am not yet ascended to
My father.*   John 20:17

T hese are the first words of the risen Christ; they strike one as
being singularly cold and repellent at such a time. Their immediate purpose was to put a barrier between Himself and Mary's
clasping hands. It was not like Him to reject tokens of love, or
to chill hearts. He had let a much worse woman than Mary
Magdalene wash His feet with tears, and wipe them with the
hairs of her head. At such a meeting, after such a parting, a little
exuberance of demonstration might have been permitted, and
forgiven even if it had been excessive.

The prohibition, strange as it sounds, was followed by a reason which sounds even more strange to our ears: "Touch Me
not; for I have not yet ascended." We might have expected that
the first "not" would have been left out, "Touch Me; for I have
not yet ascended." This would have been intelligible, as suggest-
ing that for a little time still such tokens of love were possible,
before the great separation came. Mary must have been as much

bewildered by the reason as she must have been chilled by the prohibition. And yet both were meant to lead her, with gentle, loving, and yet most firm hand, to recognize the new relation which had begun, and was henceforth to continue.

His words said to her, "old things have passed away, all things have become new," and though you have "known Christ after the flesh, yet now henceforth" (2 Cor. 5:16) you will "know Him" so "no more." They were not meant for Mary only. All the Resurrection histories have a forward look, and were intended to explain directly to the disciples, and more remotely to us, the essential nature of that new relationship into which His disciples had entered, and in which they now continued, to their Lord.

These teachings, whether expressed in words or in the facts of our Lord's appearances, are the lesson-book for the Church "till He come" (1 Cor. 11:26), and if we understand the bearings of these, we have enough to direct and to sustain us. We have, then, to deal with the three points here: the touch that was forbidden; the touch that is possible because Christ has ascended; and the lessons for today that come from both.

Then let us think of

THE TOUCH THAT WAS FORBIDDEN

This prohibition which, as I have pointed out, sounds at first repellent and cold, can only be understood if we grasp firmly and see clearly the mood and character of the person to whom it was addressed. And so I venture to turn to the circumstances that precede these words, not with any foolish ideas of telling over again the story that John has told for all time, but only for the sake of bringing out what his narrative shows us of the disposition of Mary.

I would only make one remark in passing: if this episode is not the simple recounting of historical facts, the man who wrote it must have been one of the greatest imaginative geniuses the world has ever seen. If it is not history, I would match the story of Mary and the Lord on the resurrection morning, for subtlety of characterization, for exquisite beauty, for reticence, for simplicity that goes straight to the heart, against anything that a Shakespeare or a Dante ever wrote.

But, passing altogether from that, let me just recall to you the points bearing on Mary's mood. She had visited the grave once already, found it empty, rushed away to Peter and John with the lament which henceforward became a kind of refrain upon her lips, and filled her whole heart: "They have taken away the Lord . . . we know not where they have laid Him" (John 20:2).

The two apostles ran to the tomb. She seems to have come, not with them, but after them. Manlike, they satisfied themselves of the fact and went away. Womanlike, she hung about the place, unable to tear herself from it, and yet, since the grave was empty, having no reason for staying. So, utterly absorbed in her grief, she stands there, looks into the tomb, sees the two angels as though she did not see, listlessly looks at them, and is not surprised to see them.

What were angels or anything to a woman with such a grief in her heart? They asked her a question which, if she had been less wrapped up in her sorrow, she would have discerned as being a veiled offer of help. We do not inquire of people why they weep unless we have sympathy that would like to dry their tears. But she does not hear the kindness in their question, and listlessly she gives them the old answer with a little difference. She had said to Peter and John, "They have taken away the Lord." She says to the angels, "They have taken away *my* Lord" (John 20:13). Her grief was beginning to be selfish. She was not thinking about what other people had lost, but about her possession of Him and her own desolation. Further, she was clinging despairingly to the bodily form. That form was what she meant by "*my* Lord." And the same identification or confusion of the person with the physical frame runs through all her words. She speaks of it as Him, over and over again.

Then, wearily impatient of the vain talk with these two who

had not touched her heart nor her wonder, she mechanically turns herself around and "saw Jesus standing" (John 20:14)—not coming. He was there; how He had come there no one knows. She does not recognize Him at first. That does not necessarily involve any change in Him. Whether there was or not is a large question that I am not going to touch. The hypothesis that there was is not needed to explain Mary's non-recognition. She looked at Him with the same listless eyes with which she had contemplated the angels; the same listless look with which I dare say most of us, in our times of sorrow, have looked at the vain shadows that pass before us.

"The gardener" was the natural person to be there, at that hour in the morning. So the one dominant thought rises again: "If thou have borne Him hence, tell me where thou hast laid Him" (John 20:14). And then, forgetting the weakness of a woman's arms, in the strength of a woman's love, she says: "I will take Him away" (John 20:15). She turned from Him— listless, self-absorbed in her grief, passionately clinging to the outward form, hopeless. And then came the one word of revelation, "Mary!" (John 20:16)—fancy the cadence in it—and the one word of recognition into which her whole soul flings itself in a swift rapture: "Rabboni! Master!" Who could *imagine* that?

But that exclamation shows the weakness as well as the strength of her faith. It reveals the inadequacy as well as the warmth of her conception of Jesus Christ. It is the old name, never recurring after the Resurrection except this one time. In using it she speaks her recognition only of the Christ who *had* been, not of the Christ who *was* then and *is* to be in the future. We must use our imaginations because the evangelist does not record (there was no need to tell them) the details. In the sudden impulse of her heart, when all these elements of which I have been speaking (listlessness, absorbing sorrow and hopeless-ness) had caught fire and blazed up into a flame, she made some eager movement to clasp Him, and make sure of Him.

Then came the beginning of the educational process, only explicable if you take all that I have been trying to sketch into account. "Touch Me not; for I have not yet ascended." What was the touch that was forbidden? On that very morning other women were permitted to clasp His feet. On that very evening He said to the apostles, in effect, "Handle Me and see." A week after He said to the doubter, "Reach hither thy hand, and thrust it into My side" (John 20:27). Why were they permitted what was forbidden to Mary? For this simple reason, that her attempt to clasp Him was the expression of a love and a faith which unduly clung to the external form, and which desired to perpetuate the vanished relationship. And so our Lord began the educational process, then and there. It is going on to this hour, to teach us, as it taught her, that "It is the Spirit that quickeneth; the flesh profiteth nothing" (John 6:63), and that the ascended Christ is to be grasped in another and a better fashion than with the clutch of clinging hands around the "blessed feet" that trod the plains of Galilee,

> And were nailed
> For our advantage, to the bitter cross.

Let us turn now in the second place to the consideration of

THE TOUCH THAT IS POSSIBLE BY REASON OF THE ASCENSION

"Touch Me not; for I have not yet ascended"; quite obviously that implies, "If I had ascended you might touch." And it points us onward and inward to the true meaning of Christ's ascension, to the true meaning of presence and absence in relation to Him, and to the true mode of union with Him. This communion is possible through faith and love, aspiration and obedience. Let me begin by pointing out what is a parallel, though an inadequate one. For us all, death and distance have a transforming, elevating effect upon our thoughts of those who, when they were beside us, did not seem to us so sweet, so great as now, when they are withdrawn from us. Such absence, it seems, "makes the heart grow fonder."

Though we entertain angels unawares many a time, they must
wing their way into the native haven, before we see how white
the wings and how fair the faces. Distance heightens the mountains, because it dwindles the knolls; and many a man who has
lived among his fellows unrecognized contradicts all laws of
perspective, and becomes greater as he recedes from us. Thus
you will find that, as a matter of history, it was the resurrection
and the ascension of Jesus Christ that elevated the apostolic
conceptions of Him, and that the flesh had been indeed, though
a means of revelation, also a veil.

It was so hard for them to believe that He with whom they
ate and drank all the time, that He who went in and out among
them was the Son of God. It was so hard to believe that He who
was so kindly with His kind was yet something *other than* His
kind. It took the commentary of the open grave, and the glory-
cloud hiding Him from their view, and of the Pentecost which
was the issue of both, to teach these men who it was that had
been walking among them. That resurrection and ascension
have, in like manner, been the schoolmasters of the Church
ever since, to teach it how to interpret the earthly life by the
heavenly glory.

But there is another thought to be taken into account besides
the consideration that, as is the case with others, though in an
infinitely higher degree—the withdrawal of the earthly reveals
the heavenly that shown through the earthly. We believe, as
Scripture teaches, that Christ's visible ascension was but the
symbol for our sight of a far more than material change, of the
passage of His humanity into the glory of the Father; and that as
a New Testament writer puts it: "He . . . ascended up far above
all heavens, that He might fill all things" (Eph. 4:10).

We misunderstand altogether the meaning of the ascension,
if we regard it as merely being a change of place. It is not a
leaving of the earth, but it is a passing into the heavens, that
He might more fully, and forever, dwell with us on earth.
Matthew and another evangelist have no word to say about
the ascension, and that is not because it did not come within

their circle of belief, but because it followed so closely and necessarily upon the resurrection. It also was the indispensable basis (not needing to be stated, but taken for granted) of continued presence. It does not mean Christ's withdrawal from us, but it means the possibility of Christ's presence with us, in higher and nobler fashion; and so it is precisely the evangelist who does not tell the fact, who gives us its issue in the great promise: "Lo, I am with you alway, even unto the end of the world" (Matt. 28:20).

If, then, we would rightly understand what that ascension to the Father means, we must see the teaching implied here. We must recognize that it is a step toward, not the absence of the Lord *from* His people, but the continual presence of the Lord *with* His people.

Such being the true meaning of ascension, such being the true meaning of presence (and it is a central Christian truth that Jesus Christ is, in no metaphor, with everyone who trusts in His name), look at the light that is cast upon the true way of clasping and clutching Him. "Touch Me not; for I have not yet ascended—" Mary's grasp, loving as it is, on those feet, sacred as they are, is less real than the clasp with which faith and love hold on to Him, and make Him their very own. By believing and by loving we grapple Him to our hearts with hooks of steel, and keep Him there as nothing else can. And the resulting unity is so deep, so sweet, so lifting in its results, so altogether blessed, as no outward possession could ever be. There is nothing to envy in those who companied with Him all the time He was here on earth. They had less than you and I may have.

One way by which we can clasp and hold Him, and hold Him fast, is very significantly suggested by the subsequent words of our Lord to Mary, "Touch Me not; . . . but go and tell My brethren." To do His errands and to spread His name is one of the best of the ways by which we can be in continual touch with the dear Lord. He Himself said, "If a man love Me, he will keep My words: and My Father will love him, and We will come unto him and make Our abode with him" (John 14:23). "Touch Me not; for I have not yet ascended," is convertible, by leaving out the two "nots," into the great privilege and duty of all Christians, "Touch Me; for I have ascended."

Lastly, there are

LESSONS FOR TODAY FLOWING RICHLY FROM THIS INCIDENT

I gather them into a sentence or two.

Here is a lesson for love that clings to earth. We all gravitate downward, and need to be exhorted to set our affections on things above, where Christ is, sitting at the right hand of God. The old watchword of the Church, "*Sursum corda*"— "Up with your hearts"—is based upon the whole course of thoughts involved in these words of my text. If I might take such a metaphor, just as some great silken globe inflated with a lighter gas, and rising toward the skies, may draw after it a set of heavy packages which only rise by being lashed to it; so the risen Christ lifts us, if we touch Him, to where He is, and we sit at the right hand of God in the heavenly places. To touch Christ loosens our fetters and bears us aloft.

Here is a lesson for hearts that sorrow. Poor Mary clung, as we all do, in our weakness, to the earthly form, and the dear old days, that she longed to perpetuate. She was taught that, though the old days were gone, better days were coming; and though the old form was to be withdrawn, a deeper union was possible. To her might have been addressed the consolation, "Perhaps He therefore departed for a season, that thou shouldest receive Him for ever" (Philem. 1:15). And some of us may find consolation in the same thought, and in believing that, as with this clinging woman and her dear Christ, so it may be with us and our loved and lost ones—that we are parted from them in the flesh that we might possess them in the spirit.

Here is a lesson for faith that makes too much of externals. There is a type of Christian love very genuine, but far too sentimental, and far too sensuous. We need to be reminded that the highest and the deepest love should have in it a consciousness of the separation, as well as of the union. We should not so much be seeking to clasp the feet as to receive the spirit of Jesus. I do not need to point out here what the true conception of what Christ's presence to the Church after the ascension is. It gives the real answer to that materialized notion of a Real Presence, as consisting in the magical substitution, by priestly efficacy, of the body of Jesus Christ for the bread of the communion. I am not going to speak of that. If you desire to be delivered from all undue dependence on externals ponder my text, "Touch Me not; for I have not yet ascended"—touch Me as ascended. And be quite sure of this, that to have Christ's presence in your heart is to have a far more real, and a far more blessed presence, than to see Him on the altar, or to place Him within your lips.

Now, let us contrast the warmth and closeness of the relation which thousands of men and women, in this as in every generation, bear to that Christ, with the tepid emotion and far-off admiration which follow all other great names of the world. Every one of them, founders of religions and all, drift away further and further into the mist, become more ghostly as the centuries pass by, and their influence diminishes.

But today, all over the world, there are men and women whose love to Jesus Christ is the warmest emotion in their hearts. Their closeness to Him is closer than that by which they adhere to husband, to wife, to child. Why is that? Because He, a venerable figure far away back in the past, did something some two thousand years ago, the benefit of which comes down to us today, upon the stream of time? No; but because He died indeed, but lives, and is with us, and that to bless us. He has not left the world, though He has ascended to the Father, any more than He left the Father when He came into the world.

We can sit with Him in the heavenly places, and He comes and works with us in the earthly places. So let us set our hearts

upon Him, and trusting in Him we will find that He is nearer
to us than ourselves, and that the ascended Christ is the present
Christ whom we can grasp in the only true clasp that knits
spirit to spirit by the hands of faith and love. He has ascended,
therefore, we can touch Him, as they could not who companied with Him while He was here among men.

The consciousness of sin, and the experience of pardon, deepen and make more operative in life the power of the Divine love. Thus, the publicans and the harlots do go into the Kingdom of God many a time before the Pharisees. So let us all be sure that even our sins and faults may be converted into stepping-stones to higher things.

3

The Denier Alone with His Lord

The Lord is risen indeed, and hath appeared to Simon.
—Luke 24:34

T he other appearances of the risen Lord to individuals on the day of Resurrection are narrated with much detail and at considerable length. John gives us the lovely account of our Lord's conversation with Mary Magdalene. Luke gives us in full detail the story of the interview with the two travelers on the road to Emmaus. There is another appearance, known to "the eleven . . . and them that were with them" (Luke 24:33) on the Resurrection evening, and enumerated by Paul in his list of the appearances of the Lord. This account was the common gospel of himself and all the others. Yet deep silence is preserved in regard to this appearance to Peter. No word escaped Peter's lips as to what passed in the conversation between the denier and his Lord. That is extremely significant.

The other appearances of the risen Lord to individuals on the day of Resurrection suggest their own reasons. He appeared first to Mary Magdalene because she loved much. The love that made a timid woman brave, and the sorrow that filled her heart, to the exclusion of everything else, drew Jesus to her.

The two on the road to Emmaus were puzzled, honest, painful seekers after truth. It was worth Christ's while to spend hours of that day of Resurrection in clearing questioning and sincere minds.

Does not this other appearance explain itself? Peter's brief spasm of cowardice and denial had changed into penitence when the Lord later looked at him. And his bitter tears were not only because of the denial, but because of the wound of that sharp arrow. We are happy if we have not felt the poisoned barb of the thought: "He will never know how ashamed and miserable I am; and His last look was reproach, and I shall never see His face any more."

To respond to, and to satisfy, love, to clear and to steady thought, to soothe the agony of a penitent, were worthy works for the risen Lord. I venture to think that such a record of the use of such a day bears historical truth on its very face. It is so absolutely unlike what myth-making or hallucination, or the excited imagination of enthusiasts would have produced, if these had been the sources of the story of the Resurrection. But apart from that, I wish in this chapter to try to gather three suggestions that come to us from this interview, and from the silence which is observed concerning them.

With regard to—

THE FACT OF THE APPEARANCE ITSELF

We can only rightly understand its precious significance, if we try to represent to ourselves the state of mind of the man to whom the experience was granted. I have already touched upon that; let me, in the briefest possible way, recapitulate. As I have said, the momentary impulse to the cowardly crime passed, and left a melted heart, true penitence, and profound sorrow. One sad day slowly wore away. Early on the next came the message which produced an effect upon Peter so great, that the gospel, which in some sense is his gospel (I mean that "according to Mark"), alone contains the record of it—the message through the open grave: "Tell [My] disciples *and Peter* that [I] goeth before you into Galilee" (Mark 16:7). There followed the sudden rush to the grave, when the feet made slow by a heavy conscience were distanced by the light step of happy love, and "the other disciple did outrun Peter" (John 20:4).

The more impulsive of the two dashed into the sepulcher, just as he afterwards threw himself over the side of the boat. There he floundered through the water to get to his Lord's feet. On the other hand, John was content with looking, just as he afterwards was content to sit in the boat and say, "It is the Lord" (John 21:7). But John's faith, too, outran Peter's, and he departed "believing," while Peter only went away "wondering." And so another day wore away, and at some unknown hour in it, Jesus stood before Peter alone.

What did that appearance say to the penitent man? Of course, it said to him what it said to all the rest, that death was conquered. It lifted his thoughts of his Master. It changed his whole atmosphere from gloom to sunshine, but it had a special message for him. It said that no fault, no denial, bars or diverts Christ's love to His follower. Peter, no doubt, as soon as the hope of the Resurrection began to dawn upon him, felt fear contending with his hope, and asked himself, "If He is risen, will He ever speak to me again?" And now here He is with a quiet look on His face that says, "Notwithstanding thy denial, see, I have come to thee."

Ah! This impulsive fault of a moment, so soon repented of, so largely excusable, is far more deserving of pardon than many of our denials. For a continuous life in contradiction to our profession is a blacker crime than a momentary fall. They who, year in and year out, call themselves Christians, and deny their profession by the whole tenor of their lives, are more deeply guilty than was the apostle. But Jesus Christ comes to us, and no sin of ours, no denial of ours, can bar His lingering, His reproachful, and yet His restoring, love and grace.

All sin is inconsistent with the Christian profession. Blessed be God; we can venture to say that no sin is incompatible with it, and none shuts off wholly the love that pours upon us all. True; we may shut it out. True; so long as the smallest or the greatest transgression is unacknowledged and unrepented, it forms a nonconducting medium around us. It isolates us from the electric touch of that gracious love. But also true; it is there hovering around us, seeking an entrance. If the door be shut, still the knocking fist is upon it, and the great heart of the Knocker is waiting to enter. Though Peter had been a denier, because he was a penitent the Master came to him. No fault, no sin, cuts us off from the love of our Lord.

And then comes the other great lesson, closely connected with this, but yet capable of being treated separately for a moment. This we gather from the fact of the interview: Jesus Christ is always near the sorrowing heart that confesses its evil! He knew of Peter's penitence, if I might so say, in the grave; and, therefore, risen, His feet hurried to comfort and to soothe him. As surely as the shepherd hears the bleat of the lost sheep in the snowdrift, as surely as the mother hears the cry of her child, so surely is a penitent heart a magnet which draws Christ, in all His potent fullness and tenderness, to itself. He who heard and knew the tears of the denier, and his repentance, when in the grave, no less hears and knows the first faint beginnings of sorrow for sin. And He bends down from His seat on the right hand of God, saying, "I dwell in the high and holy place, with him also that is of a contrite and humble spirit, to revive the spirit of the humble, and to revive the heart of the contrite" (Isa. 57:15).

No fault stands in the way of Christ's love. Christ is ever near the penitent spirit; and while the penitent one is yet a great way off, He has compassion, and runs and falls on his neck and kisses him.

Now let us look at—

THE INTERVIEW OF WHICH
WE KNOW NOTHING

We know nothing of what *did* happen; we do know what *must have* happened. There is only one way by which a burdened soul can rid itself of its burden. There is only one thing that a conscience-stricken denier can say to his Savior. And—blessed be God!—there is only one thing a Savior can say to a conscience-stricken denier.

There must have been penitence with tears; there must have been full absolution and remission. And so we are not indulging in baseless fancies when we say that we know what was said in that conversation, of which no word ever escaped the lips of either party concerned. So then, with that knowledge, just let me dwell upon one or two considerations suggested.

One is that the consciousness of Christ's love, uninterrupted by our transgression, is the mightiest power to deepen penitence and the consciousness of unworthiness. Do you not think that when the apostle saw in Christ's face, and heard from His lips, the full assurance of forgiveness, he was far more ashamed of himself than he had ever been in the hours of bitterest remorse? So long as there blends with the sense of my unworthiness any doubt about the free, full, unbroken flow of the Divine love to me, my sense of my own unworthiness is disturbed. So long as with the consciousness of fault there blends that thought—which often is used to produce the dread of consequences, the fear of punishment—my consciousness of sin is disturbed. But sweep away fear of penalty, sweep away hesitation as to the Divine love, then I am left face to face with the unmingled vision of my own evil, and ten thousand times more than ever before do I recognize how black my transgression has been.

The prophet expresses it with profound truth, "Thou mayest remember, and be confounded, and never open thy mouth any more because of thy shame, when I am pacified towards thee for all that thou hast done" (Ezek. 16:63). If you would bring a man to know how bad he is, do not brandish a whip before his face,

or talk to him about an angry God. You may tell the world of
the foolishness of a person, and his foolishness will not depart
from him. You may break a man down with violent diatribes,
and you will do little more. But set him in the sunshine of the
Divine love, and that will do more than break; it will melt the
hardest heart that no pulverizer would do anything but shatter.
The great evangelical doctrine of full and free forgiveness through
Jesus Christ produces a far more vital, vigorous, transforming
recoil from transgression than anything besides. The apostle Paul
asked: "Do we then make void the law through faith? God
forbid: yea, we establish the law" (Rom. 3:31).

Then, further, a *second* consideration may be suggested, and
that is this: the acknowledgment of sin is followed by immediate
forgiveness. Do you think that when Peter turned to his Lord,
who had come from the grave to soothe him, and said, "I have
sinned," there was any pause before He said, "and thou art
forgiven"? The only thing that keeps the Divine love from flow-
ing into a man's heart is the barrier of unforgiven, because
unrepented, sin. As soon as the acknowledgment of sin takes
away the barrier—of course, by a force as natural as gravita-
tion—the river of God's love flows into the heart.

The *consciousness of forgiveness* may be gradual; the *fact of
forgiveness* is instantaneous. And the consciousness may be as
instantaneous as the fact, though it often is not. "I believe in the
forgiveness of sins," says the Apostle's Creed; and I believe that
a person may at one moment be held and bound by the chains
of sin, and that at the next moment, as when the angel touched
the limbs of this very apostle in prison, the chains may drop
from off the ankles and wrists, and the prisoner may be free to
follow the angel into light and liberty.

Sometimes the change is instantaneous, and there is no reason why it should not be thus, experienced at this moment by
any man or woman in this world. Sometimes it is gradual. The
Arctic spring comes with a leap, and one day there is thick-
ribbed ice, and a few days after there are grass and flowers. A
like swift transformation is within the limits of possibility for any

of us, and—Blessed be God!—within the experience of a good many of us. There is no reason why it should not be that of each of us, as well as of this apostle.

Then there is one other thought that I would suggest: the man who is led through consciousness of sin and experience of uninterrupted love which is forgiveness, is thereby led into a higher and a nobler life. Peter's bitter fall, and his gracious restoration, were no small part of the equipment which made him what we see in the days after Pentecost—when the coward who had been ashamed to acknowledge his Master, and whose impulsive and self-reliant devotion passed away before a flippant servant-girl's tongue, stood before the rulers of Israel, and said: "Whether it be right in the sight of God to hearken unto you more than unto God, judge ye!" (Acts 4:19). The sense of sin, the assurance of pardon, shatter a man's unwholesome self-confidence, and develop his self-reliance based upon his trust in Jesus Christ.

The consciousness of sin, and the experience of pardon, deepen and make more operative in life the power of the Divine love. Thus, the publicans and the harlots do go into the Kingdom of God many a time before the Pharisees. So let us all be sure that even our sins and faults may be converted into stepping stones to higher things.

Lastly, notice

THE DEEP SILENCE IN WHICH THIS INTERVIEW IS SHROUDED

I have already pointed to the occupations of that Resurrection day as bearing on their face the marks of veracity. It seems to me that if the story of the Resurrection is not history, the talk between the denier and the Master would have been a great deal too tempting a subject for romancers of any kind to ignore. If you read the apocryphal gospels, you will see how eager they are to lay hold of any point in the true gospels, and spin a whole fiction of rubbish around it. And do you think they could ever have let this incident alone without spoiling it by expanding it, and putting all manner of vulgarities into their story about it? But the men who told the story were telling simple facts, and when they did not know they said nothing.

But why did Peter say nothing about it? Because nobody had anything to do with it but himself and his Master. It was his business, and no one else's. The other scene by the lake reinstated him in his office, and it was public because it concerned others also; but what passed when he was restored to his faith was of no concern to anyone but the Restorer and the restored. And so a religion which is individual experience-oriented is on very uncertain ground. The less you think about your emotions, and eminently the less you talk about them, the sounder, the truer, and the purer they will be.

Goods in a shop-window are dimmed and sun-damaged very quickly, and lose their luster. All the deep secrets of a man's life, his love for his Lord, the way in which he came to Him, his penitence for his sin, like his love for his wife, had better speak in deeds than in words to others.

Of course, while that is true on one side, we are not to forget the other side. Silence as to the secret things of my own personal experience is never to include reticence as to the fact of my Christian profession. Sometimes it is necessary, wise, and Christlike for a man to reveal his heart and say, "Of whom I am chief. Howbeit for this cause I obtained mercy" (1 Tim. 1:15,16). Sometimes there is no more mighty power to draw others to the faith than to say, "Whether He be a sinner or no, I know not: one thing I know, that, whereas I was blind, now I see" (John 9:25).

Sometimes—always—a man must use the expression of his own personal experience to emphasize his profession, and to enforce his appeals. So very touchingly, if you will turn to Peter's sermons in the Acts, you will find that he describes himself there (though he does not hint that it is himself) when he appeals to all his brethren, and says, "Ye denied the Holy One and the Just" (Acts 3:14). The personal allusion would make his voice vibrate as he spoke, and give force to the charge.

Similarly, in the letter which bears his name—the second of the two Epistles of Peter—there is one little morsel of evidence that inclines me to think it is his personal testimony. He sums up all the sins of the false teachers whom he is denouncing in this: *"denying* the Lord that bought them" (2 Peter 2:1). But with these limitations, and remembering that the statement is not one to be unconditionally and absolutely put, let the silence with regard to this interview teach us to guard the depths of our own Christian lives.

Let me ask this: Have you ever gone apart with Jesus Christ, as if He and you were alone in the world? Have you ever spread out all your denials and faults before Him? Have you ever felt the swift assurance of His forgiving love, covering over the whole heap, which dwindles as His hand lies upon it? Have you ever felt the increased loathing of yourselves which comes with the certainty that He has passed by all your sins? If you have not, you know very little about Christ, or about Christianity (if I may use the abstract word), or about yourselves; and your religion, or what you call your religion, is a very shallow, superficial, and inoperative thing.

Do not shrink from being alone with Jesus Christ. There is no better place for a guilty person, just as there is no better place for an erring child than its mother's bosom. When Peter had caught a dim glimpse of what Jesus Christ was, he cried: "Depart from me; for I am a sinful man, O Lord!" (Luke 5:8). When he knew his Savior and himself better, he clung to Him because he was so sinful. Do the same, and He will say to you: "Son, thy sins be forgiven thee" (Mark 2:5). "Daughter, thy faith hath made thee whole; go in peace, and be whole of thy plague" (Mark 5:34).

One might have expected that He would have flashed His presence upon them, and cleared up everything. Not so! They were not ready for that. They needed *instruction* before they could get *revelation*. When the instruction came, it all revolved around one point. Their error was in thinking that the death of Jesus Christ was fatal to His claims to be the Messiah, and the answer to that was to show them that the death of Jesus Christ was not fatal to, but a confirmation of, His Messianic character, and the necessary condition of His Messianic glory.

4

The Travelers to Emmaus

And it came to pass, that, while they communed together and reasoned, Jesus Himself drew near, and went with them.

—Luke 24:15

The reasons for the selection of the first witnesses of the Resurrection are partly discernible. Mary Magdalene was chosen because she loved much, and sorrowed much. Peter was chosen because sin repented always attracts Jesus. But why were these two unknown men chosen? Just because "they communed together and reasoned." They were trying to extricate themselves from the labyrinth of perplexity in which they were involved, and a seeking *mind* is as sure to find Jesus as a seeking *heart*.

The comparison between the appearance to Mary, and that to the two travelers on the road to Emmaus, seems to me to throw a great light upon both the incidents. The one picture is all suffused with a rosy glow of emotion, like the dawn; the other is full of the uncolored light of calm thought. In the one, a word, "Mary" (John 20:16), reveals the Master; in the other, the revelation is put almost in the background, and instruction takes the foremost place.

Some of us apprehend Christ best by feeling, some of us by reason. It is as worthy of Him, and He counts it as fit an employment of Easter Day, to spend hours in clearing the minds of two humble gropers after truth, as to satisfy the yearnings of a heart.

Now, it seems to me that this whole story carries in it for us all great lessons, and that we shall best apprehend these by noting what I have already said is a peculiarity of the incident, i.e., that the foreground is filled by instruction, and that the actual manifestation comes at the end, and is almost, if one might say so, subordinate. We have to distinguish these two stages: the *instruction* by the way, and the *revelation* in the house. Let me deal with them, and try to draw the lessons from them.

First, then, we have to look at

THE INSTRUCTION BY THE WAY

A very important point here, I think, is the people to whom the anonymity of the instruction was given. They were not apostles, for the evangelist takes care to tell us that, while they were on the road back from Emmaus, "the eleven" (Luke 24:33) were at Jerusalem. They were so insignificant, so evidently merely belonging to the rank and file of the disciples, that the evangelist does not seem to know the name of one of them, and the other whom he does name never appears again. Yet to these two perfectly insignificant people, Jesus Christ, with the experience of death and resurrection fresh upon Him, thought it worth His while to come, to enlighten their understandings, and clear up their thoughts.

Is this not a revelation, in fact, of an eternal law, that is as true today as it was then? He who let Himself be stopped on His road to the cross by a blind beggar in Jericho, and who came and joined Himself to these two conversing on the road, will come to the poorest and weakest among us, and will help us to unravel the tangled skein of our difficulties, and to bear the burden of our sorrows, if only we will let Him. This truth is part of the message of the Resurrection: the risen Lord joyfully companies with the humblest seeker after light!

And then, if we go a step further, and look at the disposition and temper of the men which drew Him, we get further instruction. The question, with which the stranger who joined Himself to the two broke the ice, passed the usual bounds of courtesy. A chance companion had no right to know what they were talking about. But there was something in the question that evidently showed it was not curiosity, but sympathy, which prompted it. There was a proffer of help underlying it.

The naïve answer of Cleopas—"Art thou only a stranger in Jerusalem, and hast not known the things which are come to pass there in these days?" (Luke 24:18)—forgets that though the pedestrian who had joined the pair might have known about the crucifixion, He could not know that they were speaking of it. But the repeated question—in one word in the original—"what things?" (Luke 24:19)—was like the touch of the button that sends the gush of the light out, like the turning of the tap that lets the flood come. For it was answered by the long, voluble, eager statement, which reveals to us the condition of mind of these two men.

They had, as it were, two strands of thought in their minds at once, and their effort was to try and braid them together. On the one hand, there was Christ's death. That left intact their belief that He was "a prophet" (Luke 24:19), for it was part of a prophet's *role* to die. But it shattered to atoms their belief that He had been the Messiah. And there is an infinite depth of despondency, of "throwing in the sponge," of giving up the whole thing, in that word, "we trusted that it had been He which should have redeemed Israel" (Luke 24:21).

Contrast that with Mary's "they have taken away my Lord, and I know not where they have laid Him" (John 20:13). She was crushed with sorrow at the death of the Beloved; they were mourning not so much for a dead Jesus, as for the death of their own hopes. They were lamenting not the departure of a beloved

Friend, but the fall of a Leader; and with the fall of a Leader, the loss of a cause.

And now notice the nature of that utter despondency which perhaps had put into their minds the notion of beginning to desert, and of going away to Emmaus, when they should have stopped at Jerusalem. It was the beginning of a process which would certainly have gone on, unless something had come in the way to stop it.

Why was it that when the Shepherd was smitten, the sheep were *not* scattered? Here is the beginning of the scattering; why did it not go on? "We *trusted*"—how did it come that in forty days they were trusting in that Man more than ever? How was it that when the Leader fell, the cause did not collapse? How was it that it did not befall to the disciples of Jesus the Nazarene, as it befell to the disciples of that "Theudas who boasted himself to be somebody," and when "he was slain his disciples were dispersed" (see Acts 5:36), and the revolt came to an end? How? Because Jesus rose from the dead. Deny the Resurrection, and you cannot account for the existence of the Church.

Such was the one strand of their thoughts. The other opposite strand, so to speak, which, as I said, they were trying to braid into the former, came from the reports of the Resurrection. Look how incredulous they are. "A woman said"; "the angel said." Reports of a report; it is all hearsay. And then comes the staggering fact, ". . . but they were kept from recognizing him" (Luke 24:16 NIV). This extinguishes the faint glimmer of hope. Ah! if they had not been in such a hurry to leave Jerusalem after the news of messages by angels, and the visit of Peter to the grave, if they had stopped an hour or two longer, Mary would have come into the upper room; and instead of their having to commune and question with one another as to what these things could mean, they would have *seen* what they did mean. We often rack our brains to understand half-finished facts, when, if we had exercised patience, and waited in the right place for a little longer, they would have cleared themselves.

So we come to the Lord's answer. One might have expected

that He would have flashed His presence upon them, and cleared up everything. Not so! They were not ready for that. They needed *instruction* before they could get *revelation*. When the instruction came, it all revolved around one point. Their error was in thinking that the death of Jesus Christ was fatal to His claims to be the Messiah. The answer to that was to show them that the death of Jesus Christ was not fatal to, but a confirmation of, His Messianic character, and the necessary condition of His Messianic glory.

Although in a different way, yet just as really as with these two wayfarers, in this generation the death of Christ is misunderstood. We need—the Church needs, and the world needs—still more, the teaching of that Easter Day on the road to Emmaus, that the cross, which is the stumbling-block, is the very center of the Messianic work; and that He came to die, "and to give His life a ransom for many" (Matt. 20:28; Mark 10:45). You will never understand the Resurrection; you will never believe the Resurrection, to any useful purpose, unless you discern, first, the meaning of the death, and have learned that, therein and thereby, the world's sins were borne by Him. He was crucified for our offenses, and raised again for our justification. The preliminary prerequisite of profitable meditation on the Resurrection of Jesus Christ is the understanding of the mystery and meaning of His cross.

Let me draw another lesson here, not less relevant to the present, and some of its burning questions; and that is, that we do not understand the Old unless we recognize in it the introduction to the New. You may hold any theory you like, the most advanced that you can find, about the origin and date and method of composition of the Old Testament. I care very little, except as a matter of literary criticism, about the conclusions that you may draw as to that. I ask only that you see what is written plain upon that whole set of books—which are not only a set of books, but a Book, an organic whole—"the testimony of Jesus is the spirit of prophecy" (Rev. 19:10). Through them all "one increasing purpose runs."

In them is a developed Revelation, converging from all sides and all points of the horizon, on the one Person, the Incarnate Son of God, and on the one fact of the cross on which He bare the sins of the world. That is the underlying meaning. Without this perception, learning and ingenuity and criticism may be expended on the Old Testament for evermore, and yet its true glory never be discovered. So much, then, for the instruction by the way.

Now, let me say a word about the second part of this incident:

THE REVELATION IN THE HOUSE

"He made as though He would have gone further" (Luke 24:28). That was no make-believe. A chance companion picked up on the road must necessarily part company when they arrive at the house-door, unless he is invited in. They ask Him to enter, partly because they did not wish to lose His companionship; and quite as much because they did not think that it would be hospitable to let Him go along the dark road by Himself.

In recompense for His instruction they offer Him the hospitality of the humble home to which they are going. Jesus Christ would have gone on if He had not been asked to stop. *There* is a revelation, again in concrete fact, of one of the conditions of His communion and fellowship with us, now that He is the risen Lord. *He does not abide with us uninvited.* He came to these two unasked, because their comments and questions drew Him. He will not abide with them uninvited, for their not asking would show that they do not care to have Him.

If you and I wish to have His presence continuous with us, we must invite His presence. We must invite Him by desire; we must invite Him by the opening of our hearts to His entrance; we must invite Him by clearing out of the house, into which we ask Him to come, all foul things. Bees will desert a hive if there is the corpse of some animal in it. Doves will not hover above polluted fields of slain. It is of no use to say to Jesus, "Abide with us" (Luke 24:29), if we do not clear a space for Him in our hearts. If we do so, He will come. Uninvited He will pass on.

Where Jesus is welcomed as a guest He becomes host. It was a strange piece of impoliteness for the Visitor to take the chief place at the table, and begin to break the bread, and bless, and give it to the two. How they must have looked at Him when He was doing this strange thing! And then, "in the breaking of the bread," not merely at, but by that means, He was known to them. I am not dealing with the question as to how the revelation was effected. There seems to have been the removal of some subjective hindrances in themselves, because Luke says, "their eyes were opened" (24:31). But there may have been something in His action which reminded them of the blessed old days when they had often sat at table with Him, which may have sharpened their perceptions and revealed Him to them.

Be that as it may, here is another revelation, in fact, of an eternal law. If I open my heart to His knock, and invite Him in, He will sup with me, for it was their bread that He took; and I shall sup with Him, for He will make Himself the Host, and impart to me the necessary provisions for body, mind, and heart. Take Christ into your heart, and He will take the mastery of the heart, and will declare Himself to be its Lord. Take Christ into your heart, and He will not come there empty-handed, but will impart to you the bread of life.

They who know the risen Christ do not need His bodily presence. "Their eyes were opened," and the opened eyes lost the sun. Yes, just because they were opened. The lesson to be taught during those forty days of how to do without the dear Presence as they hitherto experienced it, was begun at once. Precisely as to Mary the loving, He said, "Touch Me not; for I am not yet ascended," so to the two inquirers, as soon as their instruction was completed, "and they knew Him" (Luke 24:31) risen, He passed from their sight. "It was expedient for" them, that He should "go away" (John 16:7). And thus we are lifted even by the story of the corporeal presence of the risen Lord into that higher region in which it is the privilege of the Church

to live today, where communion does not depend upon anything external, and where, though present with the body, and in
that sense absent from the Lord, we may have Christ ever with
us, till we will depart "to be with Christ, which is far better"
(Phil. 1:23).

The last thought here is this: they who know that the Lord is
risen are thereby made witnesses of His Resurrection. The two
were weary. They had traveled a day's journey, they were hungry. They had just sat down to the supper-table. The meal was
scarcely begun. Night had fallen; the darkness was upon them.
But they looked at one another, and said, "This is a day of good
tidings; we cannot hold our peace. Let us go back to Jerusalem,"
and at once they sprang to their feet and set out on the road.
The men who have known the risen Lord become His witnesses. You and I ought to be that.

I have been very imperfectly trying not to tell the story over
again, but to gather the meanings of the various events. The
story lends itself quite naturally and beautifully to the use that is
so often made of it. It is a symbol of our lives, of what they may
become. If we will, Jesus will join Himself to our company. He
will walk with us by the way. He will encourage us to tell Him
all our intellectual perplexities, as well as all our sorrows and
difficulties. He will cast His own light upon the word.

If we desire, He will come with us into our house. He will sit
with us at the table. He will provide things necessary for the body
and the soul. When the shadows begin to fall, and life's twilight
gathers blackness, He will abide with us, and bring us to that
eternal Home where we will sit at His table in His Kingdom.
There with newly opened eyes we will "see Him as He is" (1 John
3:2), and "know even as we are known." Nor will He ever vanish
from our sight, nor shall we go out from it anymore forever.

Help us, O Lord, we beseech You, that we may walk with
Jesus for our Forerunner, with Him for our Pattern, with Him for
our Companion, with Him for our goal and end! And give us
grace to live, day by day, in the sweet companionship which
clears all difficulties and satisfies all hearts!

True, the outstretched hand is nothing, unless the giving hand is stretched out too. True, the open palm and the clutching fingers remain empty, unless the open palm above drops the gift. But also true, things in the spiritual realm that are given must be asked for, because asking opens the heart for their entrance. True, that gift was given once for all, and continuously, but the appropriation and the continual possession of it largely depend upon ourselves.

5

The Risen Lord's Charge and Gift

Then said Jesus to them again, Peace be unto you: as My Father hath sent Me, even so send I you. And when He had said this, He breathed on them, and saith unto them, Receive ye the Holy Ghost: Whose soever sins ye remit, they are remitted unto them; and whose soever sins ye retain, they are retained.   —John 20:21-23

The day of the Resurrection had been full of strange rumors and growing excitement. As evening fell, some of the disciples, at any rate, gathered together, probably in the upper room. They were brave, for in spite of the Jews they dared to assemble; but they were timid, for they barred themselves in "for fear of the Jews" (John 20:19). No doubt in little groups they were eagerly discussing what had happened that day.

Fuel was added to the fire by the return of the two from Emmaus. And then, at once, the buzz of conversation ceased, for "He Himself, with His human air," stood there in the midst, with the quiet greeting on His lips. It might have come from any casual stranger, and minimized the separation that was now ending: "Peace be unto you."

We have two accounts of that evening's interview which remarkably supplement each other. They deal with two different parts of it. John begins where Luke ends. The latter evangelist dwells mainly on the disciple's fears that it was some ghostly appearance which they saw, and on the removal of these by the sight, and perhaps the touch, of the hands and the feet. John says nothing of the terror, but Luke's account explains John's statement that "He showed them His hands and His side," and that, "Then were the disciples glad" (John 20:20), the joy expelling the fear.

Luke's account also, by dwelling on the first part of the interview, explains what else is unexplained in John's narrative, i.e., the repetition of the salutation, "Peace be unto you." Our Lord thereby marked off the previous portion of the conversation as being separate, and a whole in itself. Their doubts were dissipated, and now something else was to begin. They who were sure of the risen Lord, and had had communion with Him, were capable of receiving a deeper peace, and so "Jesus said to them again, Peace be unto you"; and thereby inaugurated the second part of the interview.

Luke's account also helps us in another and very important way. John simply says that "the disciples were gathered together," and that might mean the eleven. Luke is more specific, and tells us what is of prime importance for understanding the whole incident: that "the eleven . . . and them that were with them" were assembled (Luke 24:33). This interview, the crown of the appearances on Easter Day, is marked as being an interview with the assembled body of disciples, whom the Lord, having scattered their doubts, and laid the deep benediction of His peace upon their hearts, then goes on to invest with a sacred mission, "As My Father hath sent Me, even so send I you"; to equip them with the needed power, "receive ye the Holy Ghost"; and to unfold to them the solemn issues of their work, "Whose soever sins ye remit, they are remitted unto them; and whose soever sins ye retain they are retained." The message of that Easter evening is for us all; and so I ask you to look at these three points:

THE CHRISTIAN MISSION

I have already said that the clear understanding of the persons to whom the words were spoken goes far to interpret the significance of the words. Here we have, at the very beginning, the great thought that every Christian is sent by Jesus. The possession of what preceded this charge is the thing, and the only thing, that fits a person to receive it. Whoever possesses these is thereby sent into the world as being Christ's envoy and representative. What were these preceding experiences?

The vision of the risen Christ, the touch of His hands, the peace that He breathed over believing souls, the gladness that sprang like a sunny fountain in the hearts that had been so dry and dark. Those things constituted the disciples' qualification for being sent, and these things were themselves—even apart from the Master's words—their sending out on their future life's-work. Thus, whoever has seen the Lord, has been in touch with Him, and has felt his heart filled with gladness, is the recipient of this great commission. There is no question here of the prerogative of a class or gender, nor of the functions of an order; it is a question of the universal aspect of the Christian life in its relation to the Master who sends, and the world into which it is sent.

We Protestants pride ourselves upon our freedom from what we call sacerdotalism. And we are quite willing to assert the priesthood of the believer in opposition to the claims of a class, and are as willing to forget it, should the question of the duties of the priest come into view. Some do not believe in priests, but a great many believe that it is ministers who are "sent," and that they have no charge. Officialism is the dry-rot of all the churches, and it is found as rampant among democratic free churches as among the more hierarchical communities. We are all included in Christ's words of sending on this errand, if we are included in this greeting of "Peace be unto you." "I send," not the clerical order, not the priest, but "you," because you have seen the Lord, and been glad, and heard the low whisper of His benediction creeping into your hearts.

Note, too, how our Lord reveals much of Himself, as well as of our position, when He thus speaks. For He assumes here the royal tone, and claims to possess as absolute an authority over the lives and work of all Christian people as the Father exercised when He sent the Son. But we must further ask ourselves the question, what is the parallel that our Lord here draws, not only between His action in sending us, and the Father's action in sending Him, but also between the attitude of the Son who was sent, and of the disciples whom He sends? The answer is this—the work of Jesus Christ is continued by, prolonged in, and carried on henceforward through, the work that He lays upon His servants. Notice the exact expression that our Lord here uses. "As My Father *hath* sent." That is a past action, continuing in its consequences in the present. It is not "as My Father *did* send once," but as "My Father *hath* sent," which means "is also at present sending," and continues to send.

Translating this into less technical phraseology, we here have our Lord presenting to us the thought that, though in a new form, His work continues during the ages, and is now being wrought through His servants. What He does by another, He does by Himself. And we Christian men and women do not understand our function in the world, unless we have realized this: "Now then we are ambassadors for Christ" (2 Cor. 5:20), and His interests and His work are entrusted to our hands.

How will the servants continue and carry on the work of the Master? The chief way to do it is by proclaiming everywhere that finished work on which the world's hopes depend. But note—"*as* My Father hath sent Me, *so* send I you"—then we are not only to carry on His work in the world, but if one might venture to say so, we are to reproduce His attitude toward God and the world. He was sent to be "the Light of the world" (John

8:12; 9:5); and so are we. He was sent to "seek and to save that which was lost" (Luke 19:10); and so are we. He was sent not to do His own will, but the will of the Father who sent Him; so are we. He took upon Himself with all cheerfulness the office to which He was appointed, and said, "My meat is to do the will of Him that sent Me, and to finish His work" (John 4:34); and that must be our voice too. He was sent to pity, to look upon the multitudes with compassion, to carry to them the healing of His touch, and the sympathy of His heart; so must we.

We are the representatives of Jesus Christ, and if I might dare to use such a phrase, He is to be incarnated again in the hearts, and manifested again in the lives, of His servants. Many weak eyes, that would be dazzled and hurt if they were to gaze on the sun, may look at the clouds cradled by its side, and dyed with its luster, and learn something of the radiance and the glory of the illuminating light from the illuminated vapor. And thus, "as My Father hath sent Me, even so send I you."

Now let us turn to

THE CHRISTIAN EQUIPMENT

"He breathed on them, and said unto them, Receive ye the Holy Ghost!" The symbolical action reminds us of the Creation story, when into man's nostrils was breathed the breath of life, and man became a living soul. This is but a symbol, but what it teaches us is that every Christian man who has passed through the experiences which make him Christ's envoy, receives the equipment of a new life. And that life is the gift of the risen Lord. This Prometheus came from the dead with the spark of life guarded in His pierced hands, and He bestowed it upon us; for the Spirit of life, which is the Spirit of Christ, is granted to all Christians. We have not lived up to the realities of our Christian confession unless into our death has come, and *there* abides, this life derived from Jesus Himself, the communication of which goes along with all faith in Him.

But the gift which Jesus brought to that group of timid disciples in the upper room did not make superfluous the further gift on the day of Pentecost. The communication of the Divine Spirit to the disciples runs parallel with, depends on, and follows, the revelation of Divine truth. Thus, the ascended Lord gave more of that life to the disciples. They had been made capable of more of it by the fact of beholding His ascension, than the risen Lord could give on that Easter Day. But while there are measures and degrees, the life is given to every believer in correspondence with the clearness and the contents of his faith.

It is the power that will fit any of us for the work for which we are sent into the world. If we are here to represent Jesus Christ, and if it is true of us that "as He is, so are we in this world" (1 John 4:17), that likeness can only come about as we receive into our spirits a kindred life which will effervesce and manifest itself to those around us in kindred beauty of foliage and of fruit. If we are to be the lights of the world, our lamps must be red with oil. If we are to be Christ's representatives, we must have Christ's life in us.

Here, too, is the only source of strength and life to us Christian people, when we look at the difficulties of our task and measure our own feebleness against the work that lies before us. Have you ever tried honestly to be what Christ wished you to be amidst your fellows, whether as preacher or teacher or guide in any fashion? If so, have you not hundreds of times clasped your hands in all but despair, and said, "Who is sufficient for these things?" (2 Cor. 2:16). That is the spirit into which the power will come. The rivers run in the valleys, and the lowly sense of our own unfitness for the task presses upon us, and demands to be done. These pressures make us capable of receiving that Divine gift.

It is for lack of this zeal that so much of so-called "Christian effort" comes to nothing. The priests may pile the wood upon the altar, and surround it all day long with vain cries, and nothing happens. It is not till the fire comes down from Heaven that sacrifice and altar and wood and water in the trench are licked

up and converted into fiery light. So, it is because the Christian
Church as a whole, and we as individual members of it, so
imperfectly realize the A B C of our faith, our absolute dependence on the inbreathed life of Jesus Christ, that so much of our
work is merely ploughing the sands. So often we labor in vain
and spend our strength for nothing. What is the use of a mill full
of spindles and looms until the fire-born impulse comes rushing
through the pipes? Then they begin to move.

Let me remind you, too, that the words which our Lord
here employs about these great gifts, when accurately examined, do lead us to the thought that we, even we, are not
altogether passive in the reception of that gift. For the expression, "*Receive* ye the Holy Ghost" might, with more
completeness, be rendered "*take* ye the Holy Ghost." True,
the outstretched hand is nothing, unless the giving hand is
stretched out too. True, the open palm and the clutching
fingers remain empty, unless the open palm above drops the
gift. But also true, things in the spiritual realm that are given
must be asked for, because asking opens the heart for their
entrance. True, that gift was given once for all, and continuously, but the appropriation and the continual possession of
it largely depend upon ourselves.

There must be *desire* before there can be *possession*. If a man
does not take his pitcher to the fountain the pitcher remains
empty, though the fountain never ceases to spring. There must
be taking by patient waiting. The old Quaker Friends have a
lovely phrase when they speak about "waiting for the springing
of the life." If we hold out a tremulous hand, and our cup is not
kept steady, the falling water will not enter it, and much will be
spilled upon the ground. Wait on the Lord, and the life will rise
like a tide in the heart. There must be a taking by the faithful
use of what we possess.

"Unto every one which hath shall be given" (Luke 19:26).
There must be a taking by careful avoidance of what would
hinder. In the winter weather the water supply sometimes fails
in a house. Why? Because ice plugs the service-pipe. Some of us

have a plug of ice, and so the water has not come. "*Take* the Holy Spirit!"

Now, lastly, we have here

THE CHRISTIAN POWER OVER SIN

I am not going to enter into controversy here. The words which close our Lord's great charge here have been much misunderstood by being restricted. It is eminently necessary to remember here that they were spoken to the whole community of Christian souls. The harm that has been done by their restriction to the so-called priestly function of absolution has been extensive. Large effects follow from the Christian discharge by all believers of the office of representing Jesus Christ.

We must interpret these words in harmony with the two preceding points, the Christian mission and the Christian equipment. So interpreted, they lead us to a very plain thought which I may put thus. This same apostle tells us in his letter that "[Jesus Christ] was manifested to take away our sins" (1 John 3:5). His work in this world, which we are to continue, was to put away sin by the sacrifice of Himself. We continue that work when we do all that we as Christians have the right to do—we lift up our voices with triumphant confidence, and call upon others to "behold the Lamb of God which taketh away the sin of the world" (John 1:29). The proclamation has a twofold effect, according as it is received or rejected; to him who receives it, his sins melt away, and the preacher of forgiveness through Christ has the right to say to his brother, "Your sins are forgiven because you believe on Him." The rejecter or the neglecter binds his sin upon himself by his rejection or neglect. The same message is, as the apostle puts it, "the savor of death unto death; and to the other the savor of life unto life" (2 Cor. 2:16).

These words are the best commentary on this part of my text. The same heat, as the old fathers used to say, "softens wax and hardens clay." The message of the word will either heal a blind eye, and let in the light, or draw another film of obscurity over it.

And so, Christian men and women have to feel that to them is entrusted a solemn message. They walk in the world charged with a mighty power, and by the preaching of the Word, and by their own utterance of the forgiving mercy of the Lord Jesus, they may "remit" or "retain" not only the punishment of sin, but sin itself. How tender, how diligent, how reverent, how—not bowed down but—erect under the weight of our obligations, we should be, if we realized that solemn thought!

He is called "doubting Thomas." He was no doubter. Flat, frank, dogged disbelief, and not hesitation or doubt, was his attitude. The very form in which he puts his requirement shows how he was hugging his unbelief, and how he had no idea that what he asked would ever be granted. "Unless I have so-and-so I will not," indicates an altogether different spiritual attitude from what "If I have so-and-so, I will," would have indicated. The one is the language of willingness to be persuaded, the other is the token of a determination to be obstinate.

6

Thomas and Jesus

And after eight days again His disciples were within, and Thomas with them: then came Jesus. —John 20:26

There is nothing more remarkable about the narrative of the Resurrection, taken as a whole, than the completeness with which our Lord's appearances met all varieties of temperament, condition, and spiritual standing. Mary, the lover; Peter, the penitent; the two disciples on the way to Emmaus, the thinkers; Thomas, the stiff unbeliever. The presence of the Christ is enough for them all; it cures those who need curing, and gladdens those who need gladdening.

I am not going to do anything so foolish as to try to tell over again, less vividly, this well-known story. We all remember its outlines, I suppose: The absence of Thomas from Christ's first meeting with the assembled disciples on Easter evening; the dogged disbelief with which he met their testimony; his arrogant assumption of the right to lay down the conditions on which he should believe, and Christ's gracious acceptance of the conditions; the discovery when the conditions were offered that they were not necessary; the burst of glad conviction which lifted him to the loftiest height reached while Christ was on earth, and then the summing up of all in our Lord's words (John 20:29)—"Blessed are they that have not seen and yet have believed"—the last Beatitude, that links us and all the generations yet to come with the story, and is like a finger pointing to it. These contain very special lessons for them—and us—all.

I simply seek to bring out the force and instructiveness of the story. The first point is—

THE ISOLATION THAT MISSES THE SIGHT OF THE CHRIST

"Thomas, one of the twelve . . . was not with them when Jesus came" (John 20:24). No reason is given. The absence may have been purely accidental, but the specification of Thomas as "one of the twelve," seems to suggest that his absence was regarded by the evangelist as a dereliction of apostolic duty; and the cause of it may be found, I think, with reasonable probability, if we take into account the two other things that the same evangelist records concerning this apostle.

One is his exclamation, "Let us also go. . . ." It shows a constitutional tendency to accept the blackest possibilities as certainties, but it blends very strangely and beautifully with an intense and brave devotion to his Master. When, a few days before the Passion, Christ announced His intention to return to the grave of Lazarus, "Then said Thomas . . . Let us also go, that we may die with Him" (John 11:16). "He is going to His death, that I am sure of, and I am going to be beside Him even in His death." Thomas was a constitutional pessimist!

The only other notice we have of him is that he broke in—with apparent irreverence which was not real—with a brusque contradiction of Christ's saying that they knew the way, and they knew His goal. "Lord! we know not whither Thou goest" (John 14:5)—there spoke pained love confronting the black prospect of eternal separation—"and how can we know the way?" (John 14:5). There spoke almost impatient despair.

So is not that the kind of man who on the Resurrection day would have been saying to himself, even more decidedly and more bitterly than the two questioning thinkers on the road to Emmaus had said it, "We *trusted* that this had been He, but it is all over now"? The keystone was struck out of the arch, and this brick tumbled away by itself. The hub was taken out of the wheel, and the spokes fell apart. The divisive tendency was begun, as I had occasion to remark in an earlier chapter.

Thomas did the very worst thing a melancholy man can do. He went away to brood in a corner by himself, and so to exaggerate all his idiosyncrasies, to distort the proportion of truth, to hug his despair, by separating himself from his fellows. Therefore, he lost what they received, the sight of the Lord. He "was not with them" when Jesus came. Would he not have been better off in the upper room than gloomily turning over in his mind the dissolution of the fair company and the shipwreck of all his hopes?

May we not learn a lesson from this? I venture to apply these words to our gatherings for worship. The worst thing that a man can do when disbelief, or doubt, or coldness shrouds his sky, and blots out the stars, is to go away by himself and shut himself up with his own, perhaps morbid, or, at all events, disturbing, thoughts. The best thing that he can do is to look for fellowship with his Christian friends. If the sermon does not do him any good, the prayers and the praises and the sense of brotherhood will help him.

If a fire is going out, pull the dying coals close together, and they will make each other break into a flame. One great reason for some of the less favorable features that modern Christianity presents, is that people are beginning to think less than they ought to do, and less than they used to do, of the obligation and the blessing, whatever their spiritual condition, of gathering together for the worship of God. But, further, there is a far wider thought than that here. I have already referred to it, and I do not need to dwell upon it. It is this: although there are plain limits to be put to the principle, yet this is a principle: solitude is not the best medicine for any disturbed or saddened soul.

It is true that solitude is the mother-country of the strong, and that unless we are accustomed to live very much alone, we shall not live very much with God. But, on the other hand, if you cut yourself off from the limiting, and therefore developing, society of your fellows, you will rust, you will become what they call eccentric. Your idiosyncrasies will swell into monstrosities, your peculiarities will not be subjected to the gracious process of pruning which society with others and especially with Christian hearts, will bring to them. And in every way you will be more likely to miss the Christ than if you were in company with your kind, and went up to the house of God together.

Now look at the next point that is here:

THE STIFF INCREDULITY THAT THOMAS EXPRESSED

When Thomas came back to his brethren, they met him with the witness that they had seen the Lord. And he met them as they had met the witnesses who brought the same message to them. They had thought the women's words "idle tales" (Luke 24:11). Thomas gives them back their own incredulity. Let me remind you of what I have already pointed out. This frank acknowledgment that none of these, who were afterwards to be witnesses of the Resurrection to the world, accepted testimony to the Resurrection as enough to convince them, enhances the worth of their testimony. It entirely shatters the conception that the belief in a Resurrection was a mist that rose from the undrained swamps of their own heated imaginations.

Notice how Thomas exaggerated their position, however, and took up a far more defiant stance than any of them had done. He is called "doubting Thomas." He was no doubter. Flat, frank, dogged *disbelief*, and not hesitation or doubt, was his attitude. The very form in which he puts his requirement shows how he was hugging his unbelief, and how he had no idea that what he asked would ever be granted. "Unless I have so-and-so I will not," indicates an altogether different spiritual attitude from what "If I have so-and-so, I will," would have indicated. The one is the language of *willingness to be persuaded,* the other is the token of *determination to be obstinate.*

What right had he—what right has any man—to say, "So-and-so must be made plain to me, or I will not accept a certain truth"? You have a right to ask for satisfactory evidence; you have no right to make up your mind beforehand what that evidence must necessarily be. Thomas showed his hand not only in the form of his expression, not only in his going beyond his province and prescribing the terms of surrender, but also in the terms which he prescribed. True, he is only saying to the other apostles, "I will give in if I have what you had," for Jesus Christ had said to them, "Handle Me and see."

Although they could thus say nothing in opposition, it is clear that he was asking more than was necessary, and more than he had any right to ask. And he shows his hand, too, in another way. "I will not believe"—what business had he, what business have we, to bring any question of will into the act of belief or credence? Thus, in all these four points, the *form* of the demand, the *fact* of the demand, the *substance* of the demand, and the *implication* in it, that to give or withhold assent was a matter to be determined by inclination, this man stands not as an example of a *doubter,* but as an example of a determined *disbeliever* and *rejecter.* There are already too many such amongst us!

So I come to the third point, and that is:

THE REVELATION THAT TURNED THE DENIER INTO A RAPTUROUS CONFESSOR

What a strange week that must have been between the two Sundays—that of the Resurrection and the next! Surely it would have been kinder if the Christ had not left the disciples, with their new-found, tremulous, raw conviction. It would have been less kind if He had been with them. For there is nothing worse for the solidity of a man's spiritual development than that it should be precipitated, and new thoughts must have time to take the shape of the mind into which they come, and to mold the shape of the mind into which they come. So they were left to quiet reflection, to meditation, to adjust their thoughts, to get to understand the bearings of the transcendent fact. And as a mother will go a little way off from her little child, in order to encourage it to try to walk, they were left alone to make experiments in that self-reliance which was also reliance on Him, and which was to be their future and their permanent condition.

So the week passed, and they became steadier and quieter, and began to be familiar with the thought, and to see some glimpses of what was involved in the mighty fact of a risen Savior. Then He comes back again, and when He comes He singles out the unbeliever, leaving the others alone for the moment, and He gives him back, granted, his arrogant conditions.

How much ashamed Thomas must have been when he heard his demands quoted by the Lord's own lips! How different they would sound from what they had sounded when, in the self-sufficiency of his obstinate determination, he had blurted them out in answer to the testimony of his fellow disciples! There is no surer way to make a good man ashamed of his wild words than just to say them over again to him when he is calm and cool. Christ's granting the request was His sharpest rebuke of the request.

But there was not only the gracious and yet chastising granting of the foolish desire, but there was a penetrating warning: "Be not faithless, but believing" (John 20:27). What did that mean? It meant this: "It is not a question of evidence, Thomas; it is a question of disposition. Your incredulity is not due to your not having enough proof to warrant your belief, but to your tendency and attitude of mind and heart." There is light enough in the sun; it is our eyes that are wrong, and deep below most questions, even of intellectual credence, lies the disposition of the man.

The ultimate truths of religion are not matters of demonstration any more than the fundamental truths of any science can be proved; any more than Euclid's axioms can be demonstrated; any more than the sense of beauty or the ear for music depend on the understanding. "Be not faithless, but believing." The eye that is sound will see the light.

And there is another lesson here. The words of our Lord, literally rendered, are, "become not faithless, but believing." There are two tendencies at work with us, and the one or the other will progressively lay hold upon us, and we will increasingly yield to it. You can cultivate the habit of incredulity until you descend into the class of the faithless; or you can cultivate the opposite habit and disposition until you rise to the high level of a settled and sovereign belief.

It is clear that Thomas did not reach forth his hand and touch. The rush of instantaneous conviction swept him along and bore him far away from the state of mind which had asked for such evidence. Our Lord's words must have pierced his heart, as he thought: *Then He was here all the while; He heard my wild words; He loves me still.* As Nathanael, when he knew that Jesus had seen him under the fig-tree, broke out with the exclamation, "Rabbi, Thou art the Son of God" (John 1:49), so Thomas, smitten as by a lightning flash with the sense of Jesus' all-embracing knowledge and all-forgiving love, forgets his incredulity and breaks into the rapturous confession, the highest ever spoken while He was on earth: "My Lord and my God" (John 20:28).

So swiftly did his whole attitude change. It was as when the eddying volumes of smoke in some great conflagration break into sudden flame, the ruddier and hotter, the blacker they were. Sight may have made Thomas believe that Jesus was risen, but it was something other and more inward than sight that opened his lips to cry, "My Lord and my God."

We note

A LAST BEATITUDE THAT EXTENDS TO ALL
GENERATIONS

"Blessed are they that have not seen, and yet have believed" (John 20:29). I need not do more than just in a sentence remind you that we shall very poorly understand either this saying or this Gospel or the greater part of the New Testament, if we do not make it very clear to our minds that "believing" is not credence only but *trust*. The object of the Christian's faith is not a proposition; it is not a dogma or a truth, but a *Person*. And the act of faith is not an acceptance of a given fact, a Resurrection or any other, as true, but it is a reaching out of the whole nature to Him and a resting upon Him.

I have said that Thomas had no right to bring the will to bear on the act of belief, considered as the intellectual act of accepting a thing as true. But Christian faith, being more than intellectual belief, does involve the activity of the will. Credence is the starting-point, but it is no more than that. There may be belief in the truth of the gospel and not a spark of faith in the Christ revealed by the gospel.

Even in regard to that lower kind of belief, the assent which does not rest on sense has its own blessing. Sometimes we are ready to think that it would have been easier to believe if "we have seen with our eyes . . . and our hands have handled, of the (incarnate) Word of Life" (1 John 1:1), but that is a mistake.

This generation, and all generations who have not seen Him, are not in a less advantageous position in regard either to credence or to trust, than were those who accompanied Him on earth. And the blessing which He breathed out in that upper room comes floating down the ages like a perfume diffused through the atmosphere. It is with us as fragrant as it was in the days of His flesh.

There is nothing in the world's history comparable to the warmth and closeness of conscious contact with that Christ, dead for nearly twenty centuries now, which is the experience today of thousands of Christian men and women. All other names pass, and as they recede through the ages, thickening veils of oblivion, mists of forgetfulness, gather around them. They melt away into the fog and are forgotten. Why is it that one Person, and one Person only, triumphs even in this respect over space and time, and is the same close Friend with whom millions of hearts are in loving touch, as He was to those who gathered around Him upon earth?

What is the blessing of this faith that does not rest on sense, and only in a small measure on testimony or credence? Part of its blessing is that it delivers us from the tyranny of sense, sets us free from the crowding oppression of "things which are seen" and "are temporal"; it draws back the veil and lets us behold "the things which are not seen" and are "eternal" (see 2 Cor. 4:18).

Faith is sight, the sight of the inward eye. It is the direct perception of the unseen. It sees Him who is invisible. The vision which is given to the eye of faith is more real in the true sense of that word, more substantial in the true sense of that word, more reliable and more near than that by which the bodily eye beholds external things. When we trust, we see greater things than when we look. The blessing of blessings is that the faith which triumphs over the things seen and temporal, brings into every life the presence of the unseen Lord.

We must not confound *credence* with *trust*. Remember that trust does involve an element of will. Ask yourselves if the things seen and temporal are great enough, lasting enough, real enough to satisfy you, and then remember whose lips said, "Become not faithless but believing," and breathed His last Beatitude upon those "who have not seen and yet have believed." We may all have that blessing lying like dew upon us, amidst the dust and scorching heat of the things seen and temporal. We will have it, if our hearts' trust is set on Him, of whom one of the listeners on that Sunday long after spoke. His words seem to echo that promise, as "(Jesus) in whom, though now ye see Him not, yet believing, ye rejoice with joy unspeakable and full of glory: Receiving the end of your faith, even the salvation of your souls" (1 Peter 1:8,9).

This is more than a parable for earth; it is a prophecy for heaven. There on the steadfast shore He welcomes His servants from their toil on the tossing sea; and when they land they come not empty-handed, but bearing with them their works that "follow them," and, as the prophet says, "they that have brought it together shall drink it in the courts of my holiness" (Isa. 62:9). So it may be with us all, if we will. We, too, toiling in the night, may be aware of a Presence that sheds peace across the waters, like a moonbeam over a stormy sea.

7

The Sea and the Beach

This is now the third time that Jesus showed Himself to His disciples, after that He was risen from the dead. —John 21:14

The risen Lord's appearances to the disciples on Easter Day were chiefly intended to enkindle and confirm their faith in the fact of the Resurrection. That being done, a pause ensued, during which they did not have His presence. They returned to Galilee, and, as it would appear—some of them at all events—to the old haunts, and there awaited the fulfillment of the promise: "There shall ye see Him" (Matt. 28:7; Mark 16:7).

My text refers to the fulfillment of that promise. The evangelist is careful to point out that this is the third of the Lord's appearances to the assembled disciples, the other two having been those on Easter Sunday itself, and a week after, mainly for the benefit of the unbelieving Thomas.

Now, there is a very obvious and striking difference between these two sets of appearances, which are thus divided by a parenthesis of absence. In the one, the object is, as I have said, mainly to demonstrate the fact of the Resurrection. In the other, the object is mainly to reveal the consequences of that fact, and to show what the risen Lord will be to His servants, where they may find Him, how they may recognize Him, and what He will do for them. Consequently, there is an obvious difference in the prominence given to the disciples in the two sets of narratives. In the former they simply appear as doubting and convinced; in the latter they play a much more prominent part.

One other observation must be made in order that we may grasp the whole meaning of this third manifestation to the assembled disciples, and that is this: It is a replica of a previous event—the time when the first apostles were called to their office by that miraculous draught of fishes by the same Sea of Tiberias. Differences occur, which are as significant as the resemblances, but this later manifestation is evidently built upon, and refers to, the former.

That former incident is by our Lord Himself declared to be symbolical of His call to the apostles to be "fishers of men" (Matt. 4:19; Mark 1:17), and we are, therefore, not only permitted, but obliged, to regard this incident, too, as having the same coloring and the same application. It is intended to be, in symbolical form, a revelation of the relation of the risen Lord to His toiling servants. In the former event He was with them in the boat; in this He stands on the firm beach while they toil on the tossing sea.

So then, there are two main points here, the toilers on the sea and the Lord on the beach, and the toilers with their Lord at the meal on the shore. Let us look at these two:

We have in the former part of the incident—

THE TOILERS ON THE SEA, AND THE LORD ON THE SHORE

A little group of seven disciples had held together, and come back, as I said, to their old haunts. The composition of the group is remarkable. Three of the seven belonged to the first set of disciples; a fourth was the disbelieving Thomas, who had had enough of solitary brooding, and now found safety in companionship; a fifth was Nathanael, and then there were two unnamed disciples. The three inseparables, Peter, James, and John, are separated in the catalog here; Peter being put first, and James and John at the end, veiled under their patronymic or surname. Does not that place of inferiority, and that half-concealed declaration of their presence on the occasion, coincide with the supposed authorship of this gospel? Who but John would have put himself at the tail-end of such a catalog as this?

"Simon Peter saith unto them, I go a fishing" (John 21:3). The man of action felt waiting to be irksome, and the rest of them fell in with his proposal. They had come to Galilee to meet Christ. It might have seemed a very dull, prosaic kind of thing to go back to the old life with nets and boats, after the excitements and the blessednesses of the three years of communion, and with such an expectation flaming in their hearts, but it was wise.

We too shall be wise if we learn that wholesome expectation of great crises should never make us disgusted with small duties. The steadying effect of sticking to humble tasks is taught us here, and the wisdom of always making our waiting, which is no small part of our work on earth, associated with active endeavor. We shall be most sure of meeting Jesus Christ in the dusty roads of common life, if we are expecting with an inward and an upward-looking eye, even while we toil and travel. It was to "shepherds . . . keeping watch over their flocks by night" (Luke 2:8) that the infant King was shown. It was to a handful of toiling fishermen in a slimy boat that the Master appeared on the shore. "I being in the way," they could say, "the Lord met me."

The night's toil had been in vain. The rising sun ended the hopes of a haul. And so it was at the very moment that disappointment would be busiest at their hearts that the Stranger was seen on the beach. His question is not adequately represented either in the Authorized or the Revised Version, for it does not refer so much to their supply of food for themselves as to the success of their fishing, and is the kind of question that a curious bystander, or an intending purchaser, would be likely to put. And the answer, curt, is such as weary fishermen with empty nets, who had something else to do than talk to a passerby, would be likely to fling over a hundred yards of water. "They answered, No." We do not need to bring in any idea of a personal change in the corporeity of Jesus Christ to understand their non-recognition of Him. It was the gray dawn of the morning; they were not thinking about Him; they had something else to look at, they scarcely looked at Him. They answered as briefly as possible, and then went on with their work.

Then came the first of the revealing words: "Cast the net on the right side of the ship, and ye shall find" (John 21:6). His statement makes it clear that the risen Christ directs His servants. The season may seem to be past, long and futile toil may have discouraged and saddened us. Hope may be nearly dead, but we must keep our hearts, as we ought to keep them, in the attitude of waiting. Sometimes though we do not so keep our hearts, and are thinking about anything else, we shall hear—by His providences, by the whispers of His Spirit to our spirits, by His shaping and directing of our own honest attempts to ascertain our duty—we shall hear Him speak.

Never fear! For this incident is no mere exhibition, in a transitory fashion, of a temporal blessing. Rather, it is the relation—not symbolically, but actually, as being the natural expression of His interest in His servants' work—of the perpetual fact that those who wait on Him to be guided *will* be guided. Our lives, all of them, are regulated by the hand of that directing Christ, who, from the safe shore, guides the tossing boats. This is no mere fanciful spiritualizing of a fact which was never meant to carry such weighty lessons. It is, instead, the discernment, beneath one incident, of the perpetual principle from which that incident flows, and from which other similar ones will flow, if we fulfill the conditions. The risen Christ, unseen, is interested in His servants' toils, and the risen Christ will guide us, if we will let ourselves be guided.

Then comes the other thought, that this guiding Christ is the

Source of success, as well as the Fountain of counsel. "They cast therefore, and now they were not able to draw it for the multitude of fishes" (John 21:6). No doubt they thought to themselves, *The Stranger there on the beach has seen some signs of a shoal from His higher elevation that we on the water's level have failed to note.* But, at all events, they obeyed, and obeying they received the result.

Success may not always come. Often it does not come so far as outward things are concerned; but true success, that of knitting my heart and will more closely to the heart and will of Jesus Christ, always does come. And when He chooses, and knows it to be best for us, the empty nets will be filled, and we will be amazed at the results of our toil.

Then, further, the risen Lord, directing and prospering the obedience of His servants, is recognized by the swift insight of love. John sits quietly in the boat, and, not because his eyes were clearest, but because his love was deepest, and his temperament reflective, he first saw behind the veil and found the Friend behind it. The same experiences happen to many of us, but some of us are blind, and some of us can see.

They who see are they who love, and they who ponder. We need to meditate upon the facts of our individual lives, and that not only for the purpose of deducing from our past experience maxims that might guide our steps to earthly success. If we did, we should more frequently be thrilled with the startling joy of discerning, in what had seemed vacancy, the Presence, and in what had seemed a Stranger, the veritable Christ Himself. And when you and I can say, looking upon some event that to others seems to be common and earthly, "It is the Lord!" then crooked things are made straight, and rough places plain; and the heart is calmed, and the muscles are braced, and work is possible, and all vigor and peace return to our happy hearts. The eye that sees the Lord amidst the whirl of earthly things, sees all that it needs for peace and power.

I need do no more than remind you of the contrast (so obvious that everybody can see it) between the disciple who is contented with vision, and the disciple, less strong in vision, but moved by the need for action. John said, "It is the Lord!" (John 21:7), and that was enough for him. Peter had not seen that it was the Lord, but to know that it was, was not enough for him. So, picking up his fisher's coat, and hastily girding himself with it, he floundered over the side of the boat in the growing light, and somehow or other, half swimming, half wading, and not knowing how, he at last reached the Master's feet.

What sent him on that unnecessary rush, when he might have sat in the boat and come with the rest? Partly temperament, the need of action, partly a touch of his old fussiness and wish to be distinguished as well as to be doing. But I think more than all, it was the remembrance of his fall, and of his secret interview on Easter Day. On the occasion of the first draught of fishes he fell at Christ's feet saying: "Go away, for I am too sinful to be in Thy presence" (see Luke 5:8). On the second occasion he cast himself at the Master's feet, and clung to Him, saying: "Let me cling to Thee, for I am too sinful to be absent from Thee." And which was the truer penitence? Let our own hearts tell us.

We have here—

THE TOILERS AND THEIR LORD TOGETHER ON THE SHORE AT THE MEAL

We read that the rest of the disciples came in more sober fashion, bringing the boat with them through the hundred yards of distance. And when they landed they saw a fire on the beach, and the materials of a simple meal. There is no need to suppose a miracle; but if it were not a miracle, who lit that fire? Who brought the fish and the bread? Jesus Christ. You may draw symbolic meaning out of the fact, but let us cling to the plain fact to begin with, that the Hands which were pierced with the nails, and were to wield the scepter of the universe, gathered together the brands for the fire, and brought there the bread and the food.

It was just what the mothers or wives of these men would have done. It was just the thing that seven fishermen, fatigued from a night's work, wet with hauling nets, hungry with the keen morning air, needed most. And is it not, in its plain, prosaic form, the bearer of a great message for us—that Jesus Christ, our risen Lord, cares for every part of His servant's nature, and for the smallest and the humblest of His servant's necessities?

The risen Savior lays the fire, and brings the food for the toilers, and that fact was meant to be, in transient form, a revelation of one part of the perpetual relations between our Lord and His disciples.

We may note, further, how here there is the servants' contribution to what the Lord had prepared: "Bring of the fish which ye have now caught" (John 21:10). Notice the fisherman's instinct in telling the extent of the catch. John had been accustomed, in the old days, to lay out his fish on the beach and count them, and he did it that morning; and he so shows us, I think, that we have here to deal with the word of a very sober-minded, unenthusiastic eye-witness. Having it as his main object to speak about the manifestation of the risen Lord, he was cool enough to count the fish before they carried some of them to the fire of coals. That does not sound much like a hot-minded enthusiast who was the slave of some hallucination. The lesson taught us is that Jesus Christ accepts, and is glad to have given to Him, by our own act, the results which His counsel and His blessing have enabled us to achieve.

About the meal on the shore itself, I have but a word to say. We cannot but note its analogies to, and its differences from former incidents, such as the Lord's Supper, or the meal at Emmaus, or the multiplication of the loaves and fishes, on the other side of the lake. But, beyond these, note just two points. First of all, this meal suggests to us how the risen Lord, even here on earth, will and does care for the needs of His servants, and gives to them not only counsel in their toil, but refreshment after it. The consequences of our obedience become the food of our spirits, and they who hear Christ's voice, and have toiled by His command, are nourished and sustained by the result of their efforts. It is the law for life. Paul said: He who will not work, "neither should he eat" (2 Thess. 3:10). In the Old Testament God said: "In the sweat of thy face shalt thou eat bread" (Gen. 3:19).

But, in the second place, this is more than a *parable* for earth; it is a *prophecy* for heaven. There on the steadfast shore He welcomes His servants from their toil on the tossing sea; and when they land they do not come empty-handed, but bearing with them their works that "follow them," and, as the prophet says, "they that have brought it together shall drink it in the courts of my holiness" (Isa. 62:9). So it may be with us all, if we will. We, too, toiling in the night, may be aware of a Presence that sheds peace across the waters, like a moonbeam over a stormy sea. We, too, if we keep our ears open, may hear the counsel and command of His directing voice. We, too, if we obey that voice when we do hear it, may be surprised with long-delayed, and therefore the more joyous success, which will turn apparent frustration into triumphant fruition.

Whether apparent success be granted to us or not, however, all faithful service bears fruit unto life eternal. And when He calls us from the wet nets and the pitching boat, on to the steadfast shore, we will not come empty-handed, but we will bear in our hands results of the consequences not so much of our toil, as of His blessing. He will accept these, and we shall eat of the fruit of our hands, and the Master Himself will gird Himself, and come forth to serve His servants.

We might have expected: "Simon, son of Jonas, are you sorry for what you did? Simon, son of Jonas, will you promise never to do it again?" No. These things will come if the other thing is there: "Lovest thou Me?" Jesus Christ requires of us, not obedience primarily, not repentance, not vows, not conduct, but a heart; and that being given, all the rest will follow.

8

Lovest Thou Me?

Jesus saith to Simon Peter, Simon, son of Jonas, lovest thou Me more than these? He saith unto Him, Yea, Lord; Thou knowest that I love Thee. He saith unto him, Feed My lambs. —John 21:15

Peter had already seen the risen Lord. There had been that interview on Easter morning, on which the seal of sacred secrecy was impressed. Standing there alone, the denier poured out his heart to his Lord, and was taken to the heart that he had wounded. Then there had been two interviews on the two successive Sundays in which the apostle, in common with his brethren, had received, as one of the group, the Lord's benediction, the Lord's gift of the Spirit, and the Lord's commission.

But something more was needed. There had been public denial, now there must be public confession. If he had slipped again into the circle of the disciples, with no special treatment or reference to his fall, it might have seemed a trivial fault to others, and even to Peter himself. And so, after that strange meal on the beach, we have this exquisitely beautiful and deeply instructive incident of the special treatment needed by the denier before he could be publicly reinstated in his office.

The meal seems to have passed in silence. That awe which hung over the disciples in all their contacts with Jesus during the forty days, lay heavily on them, and they sat there, huddled around the fire, eating silently the meal which Christ had provided. No doubt they were gazing silently at the silent Lord. What a tension of expectation there must have been as to how the oppressive silence was to be broken. How Peter's heart must have throbbed, and the others' ears been pricked up, when it was broken by the question, "Simon, son of Jonas, lovest thou Me?"! We may listen with pricked-up ears too. For we have here, in Christ's treatment of the apostle, a revelation of how He behaves to a soul conscious of its fault. And in Peter's reaction there is an illustration of how a soul, conscious of its fault, should behave to Him.

There are three stages here: the threefold question, the threefold answer, and the threefold charge. Let us look at these:

THE THREEFOLD QUESTION

The reiteration in the interrogation did not express the Master's doubt as to the veracity of the answer, nor His dissatisfaction with its terms. But it did express, and was meant, I suppose, to suggest to Peter and to the others, that the threefold denial needed to be obliterated by the threefold confession. Every black mark that had been scored deep on the page by Peter's denial needed to be covered over with the gilding or bright coloring of the triple acknowledgment. And so Peter three times having said, "I know him not!" Jesus, with a gracious violence, forced him to answer three times, "Thou knowest that I love Thee" (John 21:15-17).

The same intention to compel Peter to face his past comes out in two things besides the triple form of the question. The one is the designation by which he is addressed, "Simon, son of Jonas." This travels back, as it were, to the time before he was a disciple, and points a finger to the weak humanity before it had come under the influence of Jesus Christ. "Simon, son of Jonas," was the name he bore in the days before his discipleship. It was the name by which Jesus had addressed him, therefore, on that never-to-be-forgotten turning-point of his life, when he was first brought to Him by his brother Andrew.

It was the name by which Jesus had addressed him at the very climax of his past life when, high up, he had been able to see far; and in answer to the Lord's question, had rung out the confession: "Thou art the Christ, the Son of the living God" (Matt. 16:16). So the name by which Jesus addresses him now says to him in effect: "Remember your human weakness; remember how you were drawn to Me; remember the high-water mark of your discipleship, when I was plain before you as the Son of God, and remembering all these, answer Me—lovest thou Me?"

The same intention to drive Peter back to the wholesome remembrance of a stained past is obvious in the first form of the question. Our Lord mercifully does not persist in giving to it that form in the second and third instances: "Lovest thou Me more than these?" More than these, what? I cannot for a moment believe that this question means something so trivial and irrelevant as "Lovest thou Me more than these nets, and boats, and the fishing?" No; in accordance with the purpose that runs through the whole, of compelling Peter to reflect, it says to him, "Do you remember what you said a dozen hours before you denied Me, 'Although all shall be offended, yet will not I' (Mark 14:29)? Are you going to take that stand again? Lovest thou Me more than these, that never discredited their boasting so shamefully?"

So, here we have Jesus Christ, in His treatment of this penitent and half-restored soul, forcing a man, with merciful compulsion, to look steadfastly and long at his past sin, and to retrace the road by which he had departed so far. Every foul place he is to stop and look at, and think about. Each detail he has to bring up before his mind.

Was it not cruel of Jesus thus to take Peter by the neck, as it were, and hold him right down, close to the foul things that he had done, and say to him, "Look, look, look ever, and answer, Lovest thou Me?" No; it was not cruel; it was true kindness. Peter had never before been so abundantly and permanently penetrated by the sense of his sinfulness, as he was after that great interview. Now it was all forgiven. So long as a man is disturbed by the dread of consequences, so long as he is doubtful as to his relation to the forgiving Love, he is not in a position beneficially and sanely to consider his evil in its moral quality only. But when the conviction comes to a man, "God has forgiven you for all that you have done"; and when he can look at his own evil without the smallest disturbance rising from slavish fear of issues, then he is in a position rightly to estimate its darkness and its depth.

And there can be no better discipline for us all than to remember our faults. As we remember the awfulness of our sins, we can rejoice that God in Christ has forgotten them. The beginning of Christ's merciful treatment of the forgiven Peter is to compel him to remember, that he may learn and be ashamed.

There is another point here, in this triple question. How significant and beautiful it is that the only thing that Jesus Christ cares to ask about is the man's love! We might have expected: "Simon, son of Jonas, are you sorry for what you did? Simon, son of Jonas, will you promise never to do it again?" No. These things will come if the other thing is there: "Lovest thou Me?" Jesus Christ requires of us, not obedience primarily, not repentance, not vows, not conduct, but a heart; and that being given, all the rest will follow. This is the distinguishing characteristic of Christian morality. Jesus seeks first for the surrender of the affections, and believes, and is warranted in the belief, that if these are surrendered, all else will follow. As love is given, loyalty and service and repentance and hatred of self-will and of self-seeking will follow in its train. All the graces of human character which Christ seeks, and is ready to impart, are, as it were, but the pages and ministers of the regal love. They follow behind and swell the *retinue* of her servants.

Christ asks for love. Surely that indicates the depth of His own! In this commerce He is satisfied with nothing less, and can ask for nothing more; and He seeks for love because He *is* love, and has given love. All hearts must be burdened, as all our hearts ought to be—unless the burden has been cast off in one way—by the consciousness of our own weakness and imperfection. Surely, surely, it is a gospel that is contained in that one question addressed to a man who had gone far astray, "Simon, son of Jonas, *lovest* thou?"

Here, again, we have Jesus Christ, in His dealing with the penitent, willing to trust discredited professions. We think that one of the signs of our wisdom is that experience shall have taught us once being bit, twice to be shy; and if a man has once deceived us by flaming professions and ice-cold acts, we should never to trust him any more. And we think that is "worldly wisdom," and "the bitter fruit of earthly experience," and "sharpness," and "shrewdness," and so forth. Jesus Christ, even while reminding Peter, by that "more than these," of his utterly hollow and unreliable boasting, shows Himself ready to accept once again the words of one whose lack of veracity He had proved. Love "believeth all things, hopeth all things" (1 Cor. 13:7), Paul says. And Jesus Christ is ready to trust us when we say, "I love Thee," even though often in the past our professed love has been all disproved.

We have here, in this question, our Lord revealing Himself as willing to accept the imperfect love which a disciple can offer Him. Of course, many of you well know that there is a very remarkable play of expression here. In the first two questions the word which our Lord employs for "love" is not the same as that which appears in Peter's first two answers. Christ asks for one kind of love; Peter proffers another. I do not intend to discuss the distinction between these two apparent synonyms. The kind of love which Christ asks for is higher, nobler, less emotional, than Peter offers in reply.

And then, in the third question, our Lord, as it were, surrenders and takes Peter's own word, as if He had said, "Be it so. You shrink from professing the higher kind; I will take the lower; and I will educate and bring that up to the height that I desire you to reach." However stained and imperfect our love is, however disproved by denials, however tainted by earthly associations, Jesus Christ will accept it. Though it be but a trickle when it ought to be a torrent, still we can bring it to Him.

These are the lessons which it seems to me lie in this triple question. I have dealt with these matters at greater length, because those which follow are largely dependent upon them. But let me just turn now briefly, in the second place, to—

THE TRIPLE ANSWER

"Yea, Lord; Thou knowest that I love Thee," Peter answers. Is not that beautiful? By Christ's Resurrection, as the last of the answers shows, Peter had been led to the loftiest conception of Christ's omniscience, and regarded Him as knowing the hearts of all men. In the face of all that Jesus Christ knew about his denial and his sin, he dared to appeal to Christ's own knowledge. What a superb and all-conquering confidence in Christ's depth of knowledge and forgiveness that answer showed! He felt that Jesus could look beneath the surface of his sin, and see that below it there was, even in the midst of the denial, a heart true in its depths. It is a tremendous piece of confident appeal to the deeper knowledge, and therefore, the larger love and more abundant forgiveness, of the righteous Lord—"Thou knowest that I love Thee."

A Christian ought to be sure of his love to Jesus Christ. You do not study your conduct to infer from it your love to others. You do not study your conduct to infer from it your love to your wife, or your husband, or your parents, or your children, or your friend. Love is not a matter of inference; it is a matter of consciousness and intuition. And while self-examination is necessary for us all for many reasons, a Christian ought to be as sure that he loves Jesus Christ as he is sure that he loves the dearest upon earth.

It used to be the fashion long ago—this generation has not depth enough to keep up the fashion—for Christian people to talk as if it were a point they longed to know, whether they loved Jesus Christ or not. There is no reason why it should be a point we long to know. You know all about your love to one another, and you are sure about that. Why are you not sure about your love to Jesus Christ? "Oh, but," you say, "look at my sins and failures"; and if Peter had looked only at his sins, do you not think that the words would have stuck in his throat? He did look, but he looked in a very different way from that of trying to ascertain from his conduct whether he loved Jesus Christ or not.

Any sin is inconsistent with Christian love to Christ. Thank God we have no right to say of any sin that it is incompatible with this love! More than that; a great, gross, flagrant, sudden fall like Peter's is a great deal less inconsistent with love to Christ than are the continuously unworthy, worldly, selfish, Christ-forgetting lives of hosts of complacent, professing Christians today. White ants will eat up the carcass of a dead buffalo quicker than a lion will. And to have denied Christ once, twice, three times, in the space of an hour, and under strong temptation, is not half so bad as to call Him "Master" and "Lord," and then day by day, week in, week out, in works to deny Him. The triple answer declares to us that in spite of a man's sins he ought to be conscious of his love, and be ready to profess it when the opportunity arises.

LAST OF ALL, WE HAVE HERE THE TRIPLE COMMISSION

I do not dwell upon it at any length, because in its original form it applies especially to the apostolic office. But the general principles which underlie this threefold charge, to feed and to tend both the sheep and the lambs, may be put in a form that applies to each of us. It is this—the best token of a Christian's love to Jesus Christ is his service of man for Christ's sake. "Lovest thou Me?" "Yea! Lord," you have said; then *go* and *do*. "Feed My lambs; feed My sheep."

We need the profession of words; we need, as Peter himself enjoined at a subsequent time, to be ready to "give an answer to every man that asketh you a reason of the hope" (1 Peter 3:15), and an acknowledgment of the love, that are in us. But if you want others to believe in your love, however Jesus Christ may know it, go and work in the Master's vineyard.

The service of man is the garb of the love of God. He who loves God will love his brother also. Do not confine that thought of service, and feeding, and tending, to what we call evangelistic and religious work. That is one of its forms, but it is only one of them. Everything in which Christians can serve their fellows is to be taken by them as their worship of their Lord, and is taken by the world as the convincing proof of the reality of their love.

Love to Jesus Christ is the qualification for all such service. If we are knit to Him by true affection, which is based upon our consciousness of our own falls and evils, and our reception of His forgiving mercy, then we shall have the qualities that fit us, and the impulse that drives us, to serve and help our fellows. I do not say—God forbid!—that there is no philanthropy apart from Christian faith, but I do say that, on the wide scale, and in the long run, they who are knit to Jesus Christ by love will be those who render the greatest help to all who are afflicted, in mind, body, or estate; and that the true basis and qualification for efficient service of others is the utter surrender of our hearts to Him, who is the fountain of love and from whom comes all our power to live in the world, as the images and embodiments of the love which has saved us that we might help to save others.

We must all ask ourselves Christ's question to the denier. Let us look our past evils full in the face, that we may learn to hate them, and that we may learn more the width and the sweep of the power of His pardoning mercy. God grant that we may all be able to say, "Thou knowest all things; Thou knowest that I love Thee" (John 21:17).

I solemnly believe that one of the perils of the church of today is the restless activity which has far more machinery than it has boiler-power for; far more work than it has retiring meditation, and which, therefore, with all its energy, is but superficial, and sows much and reaps little. I do not want fewer Christian workers, but I do want more Christian meditation and prayers. I do not want less service, but the service would be better if there was more coming apart into a solitary place with Christ, and resting awhile.

9

Doing and Staying

Jesus saith unto him, If I will that he tarry (stay) till I come, what is that to thee? follow thou Me. —John 21:22

In the preceding chapter we have seen that, in the first part of this mysterious interview by the fire of coals on the shore of the lake, Peter's threefold confession obliterated his three-fold denial. It won his threefold commission and public restoration to his apostolic office. But this was not all Jesus had to say that morning to him and to the others. Turn to the second part of this mysterious interview, and note that it groups itself around three sayings of our Lord's, of which I have taken the last as my text, because it is the summing-up of the whole.

These three sayings are a *prediction*, a *command*, and a *rebuke*. The prediction is interpreted by the writer as a forecast of Peter's martyrdom. "When thou wast young, thou girdest thyself, . . . but when thou shalt be old . . . another shall gird thee, and carry thee whither thou wouldest not" (John 21:18). That prediction is attached immediately to the commission, "Feed My sheep." It indicates that the discharge of the function would inevitably lead to the death.

Then there follows the command, "Follow thou Me," which looks back to both the commission and the prediction, and sets forth Christ, the chief Shepherd, as the great Example to be followed in life by all the under-shepherds, and changes the whole aspect of martyrdom and death by making it a following of Him.

Last comes the rebuke, occasioned by a flash of Peter's old self, possibly due partly to affection, but a great deal more to impulsive curiosity: "Lord, and what shall this man do?" He said this as he saw John following himself and the Lord. That brought the answer which I have read as my text. I wish to draw out the lessons of these three sayings of our Lord. First—

A PREDICTION

The form which it takes is picturesque and striking. An hour before, Peter, as we read in this very chapter, "girt himself" with his fisher's coat, and floundered through the shoal water to get to Christ's feet. It was a characteristic action, in which the man's masterful, impulsive nature, energetic, and craving for activity as a safety-valve to his feelings, showed itself. Our Lord takes it as a specimen of the whole characteristic nature of the man, as it had been developed in the buoyant season of his youth and early manhood.

It is a picture of the energetic fisherman, impatient of passivity, strongly self-reliant, scornful of help, and inclined to yield to the impulse of a masterful will: "When thou wast young, thou girdest thyself, and walkedst whither thou wouldest: but when thou shalt be old. . . ." At this stage in life the natural force is abated, and the attrition of life has worn the energy thin. Then "thou shalt stretch forth thy hand" that did not hitherto ask for help, "and another shall gird thee." And then in the last clause comes out more plainly the purport of the whole: "shalt carry thee whither thou wouldest not." So the early, buoyant energy is enfeebled and passes into passivity and dependence. The service of life, in feeding the lambs and the sheep, is perfected by the service of suffering and the death that he should die.

Now, notice in a word the contrast that is here suggested between the strength of youth and the passiveness of old age. It is not to be overlooked, though it is not the principal thing. "Even the youth shall faint and be weary, and the young men shall utterly fail." Nature is sapped and weakened, and as a necessary result of having been young, and vigorous, and strong we become old, and tired, and feeble. But there is a secret of perpetual youth. It is possible to resist and set at defiance, in the true depths of our being, the law which weakens energy and dims eyesight. We must wait upon the Lord, from whom comes the life that has no tendency to death. From Him comes the strength that is not exhausted by being put forth, and that has no proclivity to weakness nor needs to fear exhaustion.

The supernatural strength that may pass into the life of every one of us will conquer the natural, and the winter of the year may never need to come. "Even the youth shall faint and be weary," yes; but "they that wait on the Lord shall renew their strength" (Isa. 40:31); and according to the deep saying of the Swedish seer, "The oldest angels in heaven are the youngest."

But turning from that, which is only incidental to the main message of the words before us, note how in this prediction Jesus Christ, with the utmost calmness, very matter-of-factly, as if the propriety of it was obvious, and also with the most perfect tenderness, sets a man to a task which He knows beforehand is a sentence of death. "Feed My sheep": if you do, "Another shall gird thee and carry thee whither thou wouldest not." Jesus calls for no recruits under false pretenses; He does not coax men into His service by feigned tales of advantages and outward benefits; He does not hide the possible, and in some cases the certain, issues, but says to us, "If you do as I bid you, you will have to suffer a great deal, and you may have to lay down your lives. Do it!"

What authority does He have to lay a masterful hand upon me, and to tell me that, if I have to die for Him, I am yet in the right in following Him? What authority has He? Ah! He has

this right: He died for you and me first, before He asked us to be
ready to die for Him. If we drink in the meaning and the measure of His great love for us, we will be able to turn to Him and
say: "Thou gavest Thy life for me, and here I give my life to
Thee." It is only the risen Lord who has the right to bid us die
for Him. But He has the right, and to recognize the right is to
have death abolished and life made ours forever.

In all ages there have been those who have had, like Peter, to
complete the service of activity by the service of suffering. And—
thank God!—in all ages that spring of self-surrender which is
opened and made to flow in the rockiest hearts by the recognition of Christ's great and dying love for us—in all ages, and in
this age—that spring has not failed.

There comes into my mind a missionary family who, some
years ago in a Chinese official's office, were girded and bound
and carried whither they would not. The father of the family, in
the journey from the place of capture to the place of death (a
walk of some hundreds of miles), knowing that he was going to
his grave, preached Christ at every halting-place. When the
family reached the place of execution, he and his wife, and their
little children stretched out their necks for the headsman's sword,
without reluctance and without tremor. Thank God for the
present-day martyrs of a martyred Christ!

Let us remember this. Although our physical death may not
be demanded from us, the very same connection which is shad-
owed here as existing between a life of service and a death of
suffering, in spirit and reality remains true for all Christian living. There may not be the literal death, but no man will live a
noble Christian life unless it is a dying life. Although the natural
self may not be weakened by age, the natural self must be weakened by suppression, if we are to live the life. When you and I
stretch out our hands, and let Jesus Christ gird us, and carry us
where our flesh and blood would not prefer to go, then, and only
then, can we keep His command: "Feed My lambs; Feed My
sheep." No noble life is possible unless it be a sacrificed life.
That freedom and self-reliance when we girded ourselves, and

went wherever we would, is ignoble, and is slavery. On the other hand, the surrendered life, when we stretch out our hands and let Him lead us, is freedom and blessedness. So much, then, for the first of the sayings here, the *prediction*.

Now let us turn to the second:

THE COMMAND

"And when He had spoken this, He saith unto him, Follow Me." Note that the two sayings (the one with which I have been dealing, and the one with which we have now to deal) follow each other immediately. Yet they are separated from each other. This suggests distinction and yet connection. "He said unto him, Follow Me" (Luke 5:27). From what follows in the narrative the command evidently was first meant to call Peter to come after Jesus in some change of place, leaving the little group with the apparent purpose of giving some further private communication. But while this is no doubt true, I think that we do not need to wonder whether that private communication was ever given—or what it was. It seems to me, in accordance with the symbolical turn of all the narrative, we are to regard this commandment, though it had a literal fulfillment at the moment, as in the literal fulfillment being but a symbol of the whole Christian life.

Jesus gathers up, if I may say so, in this one commandment what He had been saying before. This includes both the commission to the life of service, and the prediction of the death of martyrdom. Both of these He, as it were, brings under the scope of this commandment, and says: "As under-shepherd, follow Me in the feeding of the sheep; and as martyr, follow Me in the death that you will die."

I have pointed out in the earlier portion of this incident the allusions to past events recorded in the Gospels; and there is a distinct double allusion here to two such. It surely is not accidental that, while the first miraculous draught of fishes by the lake was followed by the command, "Come ye after Me, and I will make you fishers of men" (Mark 1:17); the second is followed by the parallel command: "Follow thou Me." That applies to following Christ in service.

Then it surely is not accidental either, that while a few hours before Calvary, Peter asked: "Why cannot I follow Thee now? I will lay down my life for Thy sake" (John 13:37), Jesus Christ should here have said, "Follow thou Me." The "afterwards," the time when he should follow Him, had begun. That applies to the "following" by laying down the life for His sake.

So we have here Jesus Christ, as always, calmly presenting Himself before us and the whole world as the realized ideal of humanity, in whom is all perfection. To be like Him is to be complete, and to imitate Him is to be tending toward perfect righteousness. "Follow thou Me" is the one sweet word that gathers up into a blessed permission the otherwise harsh, impossible, and despair-producing imperative of duty. Everything changes when, instead of saying to a man, "Do this," we say to him, "Follow Jesus Christ." It is one thing to *obey*, or to try to obey, an impersonal "ought"; it is altogether different to *imitate* a personal Christ. And power, joy, and virtue are redoubled, and more than that, multiplied tenfold, when all duty is summed up in trying to be like Him.

It is the very life-blood of love to be conformed to the beloved; and if we, instead of aiming at a cold, far-off, abstract morality, seek to shape our lives after the pattern of a loving, near, personal Jesus, surrendering completely to His control, the aspect of duty changes, and life becomes a feast and not an effort. "Follow thou Me."

When J. Wilbur Chapman was in London, he had an opportunity to meet General Booth, who at that time was past eighty years of age. Dr. Chapman listened reverently as the old general spoke of the trials and the conflicts and the victories he had experienced.

The American evangelist then asked the general if he would disclose his secret for success. "He hesitated a second," Dr. Chapman said, "and I saw the tears come into his eyes and steal down his cheeks," and then he said, "I will tell you the secret. God has had all there was of me. There have been men with greater brains than I, men with greater opportunities; but from the day I got the poor of London on my heart, and a vision of what Jesus Christ could do with the poor of London, I made up my mind that He would have all of William Booth there was. And if there is anything of power in the Salvation Army today, it is because God has all the adoration of my heart, all the power of my will, and all the influence of my life."

Dr. Chapman said he went away from that meeting with General Booth knowing "that the greatness of a man's power is the measure of his surrender."

So may it be with us. I do not dwell on the way in which this complete submission to and imitation of Christ is to be the guiding star of all men who especially are called upon to feed the sheep and the lambs. But I wish you to remember that this exhortation, regarded as being the one all-comprehensive commandment for life, does not apply only to the service of those who are shepherds. Peter himself, remembering this incident, as it seems to me, shared his privilege of following Jesus, which he had once grudged to his dearest friend and fellow-apostle John, amongst us all, when he wrote, "Leaving us an example, that ye"—all of us—"should follow His steps" (1 Peter 2:21).

The world would be revolutionized if the Church followed Jesus as Booth did. The world brings it as its gravest charge against us that we do not, and it has the right to do so. It is a good thing for us professing Christians when we hear, from the lips of the enemies, as we may hear if we will listen, the repetition of the Master's command. Go after your Lord, and you will feed His sheep, and you will touch the conscience of the world.

And now, lastly, we have here:

THE REBUKE

As I have said, it is evident that the previous command was accompanied by some motion and change of place, because

John followed the two. And it is very beautiful to notice how John does not apologize for, but vindicates as quite proper, his apparent intrusiveness, when he describes the man who ventured to follow as being "the disciple whom Jesus loved, who also leaned on His breast at supper, and said, Lord which is he that betrayeth Thee?" If these things were true of him, he had a right to believe that no confidence imparted to his special friend, Peter, could be withheld from him; and it was no intrusion, but the recognition of that bond that knit him to Christ and to Peter, that led him to link himself with the pair.

Then there comes the flash of Peter's old self, half curiosity, half affection, and the irrepressible desire to be setting everybody straight: "Lord, and what shall this man do?" (John 21:21). That brings an answer, which is a rebuke, and also the reiteration of the commandment: "If I will that he tarry (stay) till I come, what is that to thee? Follow thou Me."

Now, I do not need to dwell upon the attitude which our Lord takes here, in full conformity with the attitude which He took in the two preceding sayings, of asserting and exercising His absolute power over the life and death of a man. His "I will" kept John alive, almost to the end of the century. By the time this chapter was written, as is obvious from the words, "what death he should die" (John 12:33), Peter had long since gone, and John was left. Jesus Christ is the Lord of life and, "has the keys of death and the grave."

But apart from that, let me just remind you, in a sentence, how we have here brought into close juxtaposition and narrow compass, the perpetually recurring double manifestations of the Christian life—the life of service and the life of waiting. Peter's only notion of service was, "Lord, and what shall this man *do?*" But there is another kind of service: "If I will that he tarry." Do? Nothing; just *tarry.*

If you read the book of the Acts of the Apostles, you find John there side by side with Peter, a kind of silent shadow. He never opens his mouth. Always at hand, he is ready to back up his energetic brother, but not a word comes from his lips during all the history in that book. He waits and waits; and the years pass on, and the silence bears fruit in his Gospel without which we would be poor indeed (though we have the three epistles, and Paul, Peter, and the rest). John's Gospel, in its deep intuitions, its strong ethics, its spiritual energy, and its enthronement of love, is worthy to be, as it seems to me that it is tending to become, the last phase of the Christian creed. That is what we get from the *tarrying* apostle.

Mary and Martha are sisters; Rachel and Leah are both wives. The contemplative and the active life need each other, else the one will become indolent, subjective, diseased; and the other will become fussy and superficial, and will dry up. It is one of the hardest things in the practical guidance of an individual life to know how much is due to the one and how much to the other.

Only let us remember that the two types are both legitimate types. It is not for me to say which is the higher. But it is for me to say that the active is always tempted to find fault with the contemplative, and to call it indolence. John will let Peter serve as much as he likes; but Peter does not let John go apart and meditate. There have been ages in which the contemplative has crowded out the active, and a monastery in its most corrupt state shows the outcome of that experiment.

This age, we people in the twentieth century, is exposed to precisely the opposite danger. I solemnly believe that one of the perils of the Church of today is the restless activity which has far more machinery than it has boiler-power. It has far more work than it has retiring meditation. Because of this, with all its energy, it is but superficial, and sows much and reaps little. I do not want fewer Christian workers, but I do want more Christian meditation and prayers. I do not want less service, but the service would be better if there was more coming apart into a solitary place with Christ, and resting awhile.

This incident also has a distinct and direct application to ourselves. We hear Christ saying to us, "Lovest thou Me?" It is for us to answer, "Thou knowest that I love Thee." Then we shall hear the command, "Follow thou Me," and we shall be able, in some measure, to serve Him with our activity, and to nestle near Him in our meditation. So we will follow Him in life, and in death, and then pass into the state where "they follow the Lamb whithersoever He goeth," and where contemplation will not slacken diligence, nor labor disturb contemplation. "Lovest thou Me? Follow thou Me. Abide with Me"—these are the master-words for a noble life, a quiet death, and a glorious Eternity.

We are always tempted to think that long ago the earth was more full of God than it is today, and that away forward in the future it will again be fuller, but that this moment is comparatively empty. It seems the heavens touch the earth on the horizon in front and behind, and they are furthest above us just where we stand. But no past day had more of Christ in it than today has, and that He has gone away is the condition of His coming. He, therefore, departed for a season, that we might receive Him forever.

10

On the Mountain

Then the eleven disciples went away into Galilee, into a mountain where Jesus had appointed them. And when they saw Him, they worshiped Him: but some doubted. —Matthew 28:16,17

After that, He was seen of above five hundred brethren at once. —1 Corinthians 15:6

To infer an historian's ignorance from his silence is a short and easy, but a rash, method. Matthew has nothing to say of our Lord's appearances in Jerusalem, except in regard to that of the women in the early morning of Easter Day. But it does not follow that he was ignorant of these appearances. Imperfect knowledge may be the explanation; but the scope and design of his Gospel is much more likely to be the reason.

Matthew is emphatically the Gospel of the King of Israel. It moves, with the exception of the story of the Passion, wholly within the limits of the Galilean ministry. What more probable explanation this: the same motive which induced Jesus to select the mountain He had appointed as the scene of this meeting induced the evangelist to pass by all the other manifestations to single out this one? It was fitting that in Galilee, where He had walked in lowly gentleness, "kindly with His kind," He should assume His sovereign authority. It was fitting that in "Galilee of the Gentiles" (Matt. 4:15), that outlying and despised province, half heathen in the eyes of the narrow-minded pharisaic Jerusalem, He should proclaim the widening of His Kingdom from Israel to all nations.

If we had Matthew's words only, we should suppose that none but the eleven were present on this occasion. But it is obviously the same incident to which Paul refers when he speaks of the appearance to "five hundred brethren at once." They were the Galilean disciples who had been faithful in the days of His lowliness. Thus they were now assembled to hear His proclamation of exaltation. Apparently the meeting had been arranged beforehand. They came without Him to "the mountain where Jesus had appointed." Probably it was the same spot on which the so-called Sermon on the Mount, the first proclamation of the King, had been delivered. Now it was naturally chosen to be the scene of a yet more exalted proclamation.

A thousand tender memories and associations clustered round the spot. So we have to think of the five hundred gathered in eager expectancy; and we notice how unlike the manner of His coming is to that of the former manifestations. *Then*, suddenly, He was visibly present where a moment before He had been unseen. But *now* He gradually approaches, for the doubting and the worshiping took place "when they saw Him," and before "He came to them." I suppose we may conceive of Him as coming down the hill and drawing near to them, and then, when He stands above them, and yet close to them—else the five hundred could not have seen Him "at once"—their doubts vanish; and they listen with silent awe and love.

The words are majestic; all is regal. There is no veiled personality now, as there had been to Mary, and to the two on the road to Emmaus. There is no greeting now, as there had been in the upper chamber; no affording of a demonstration of the reality of His appearance, as there had been to Thomas and to the others. He stands among them as the King and the music of His words, deep as the roll of thunder, and sweet as musicians playing on their harps, makes all comment or paraphrase sound thin and poor. But yet so many great and precious lessons are hived in the words that we must reverently ponder them. The material is so abundant that I can but touch it in the slightest possible fashion. This great utterance of our Lord's falls into three parts: a great claim, a great commission, and a great promise.

THE GREAT CLAIM

"All power is given unto Me in heaven and in earth" (Matt. 28:18). No words can more absolutely express unconditional, unlimited authority and sovereignty. Mark the variety of the gift—"all power"; every kind of force, every kind of dominion is in His hands. Notice the sphere of sovereignty—"in heaven and in earth." If we know anything about Jesus Christ, we know that He made this claim. There is no reason, except the unwillingness of some people to admit that claim, for casting any sort of doubt upon these words. We need not make any distinction in authority between them and the rest of the words of graciousness which the whole world has taken to its heart.

But if He said this, what becomes of His right to the veneration of mankind, as the perfect example of the self-sacrificing, self-oblivious religious life? It is a mystery I cannot solve, how any man can keep his reverence for Jesus, "the sage and the humble," and refuse to believe that beneath these tremendous words there lies a solemn and solid reality and authority.

Notice, too, that there is implied a definite point of time at which this all-embracing authority was given. You will find in the Revised Version a small alteration in the reading, which makes a great difference in the sense. It reads, "All power . . . *has been* given"; and that points, as I say, to a definite period.

When was it given? Let another portion of Scripture answer the question. In Romans 1:4 Paul writes: "Declared to be the

Son of God with power . . . by the resurrection from the dead."
Then to the Man Jesus was given authority over heaven and
earth.

All the early Christian documents concur in this view of the
connection between the death and Resurrection of Jesus Christ,
and His investiture with this sovereign power. Listen to Paul
again, "Became obedient unto death, even the death of the
cross. Wherefore God also hath highly exalted Him, and given
Him a name that is above every name" (Phil. 2:8,9). Listen to
Peter, "Who . . . raised Him up from the dead, and gave Him
glory" (1 Peter 1:21).

Listen to the writer of the Epistle to the Hebrews, "We see
Jesus . . . for the suffering of death, crowned with glory and
honor" (2:9). Listen also to John, "And from Jesus Christ who is
the faithful witness, and the first begotten of the dead, and the
Prince of the kings of the earth" (Rev. 1:5). Look with his eyes
to the vision of the "Lamb as it had been slain" (Rev. 5:6),
enthroned in the midst of the throne. This unanimous consent
of the earliest Christian teachers is inexplicable on any reasonable grounds, unless there had been underlying it just the words
of our text, and the Master Himself had taught them that all
power was given to Him in heaven and in earth.

As it seems to me impossible to account for the existence of
the Church if we deny the Resurrection, so it seems to me
impossible to account for the faith of the earliest stratum of the
Christian Church without the acceptance of some such declaration as this. It had to come from the Lord Himself. And so the
hands that were pierced with the nails wield the scepter of the
Universe, and on the brow that was wounded and bleeding with
the crown of thorns is wreathed the many crowns of universal
Kinghood.

But we must notice further that in this investiture, with "all
power . . . in heaven and in earth," we have not merely the
attestation of the perfection of His obedience, the completeness
of His work, and the power of His sacrifice, but we also have the
elevation of Manhood to enthronement with Divinity. For the

new thing that came to Jesus after His resurrection was that His humanity was taken into, and became participant of, "the glory which I had with Thee before the world was" (John 17:5). Then our renewed nature, in its perfection and its sinlessness, is so related to the Divine that humanity is capable of being invested with, and bearing that "exceeding and eternal weight of glory" (2 Cor. 4:17). In that elevation of the Man Christ Jesus, we may read a prophecy, that shall not be unfulfilled, of the destiny of all those who conform to Him through faith, love, and obedience. We will finally sit down with Him on His throne, even as He is set down with the Father on His throne.

Christianity has dark and low views of human nature, and men say they are too low and too dark. It is "Nature's sternest painter," and, therefore, "its best." But if on its palette the blacks are blacker than anywhere else, its range of color is greater, and its white is more lustrous. No system so condemns human nature as it is; none thinks so glowingly of human nature as it may become. There are bass notes far down beyond the limits of the scale to which ears dulled by the world and sin and sorrow are sensitive; and there are clear, high tones, thrilling and shrilling far above the range of perception of such ears. The man who is in the lowest depths may rise with Jesus to the highest, but it must be by the same road by which the Master went. Paul writes: "If we suffer (with Him), we shall also reign with Him" (2 Tim. 2:12), and only "if." There is no other path to the Throne but the Cross. *Via crucis, via lucis*—the way of the cross is the way of light. It is to those who have accepted their Gethsemanes and their Calvarys that He appoints a kingdom, as His Father has appointed unto Him.

So much, then, for the first point here in these words; turn now to the second:

THE GREAT COMMISSION

One might have expected that the immediate inference to be drawn from "All power is given unto Me in heaven and in earth" would have been some word of encouragement and strengthening to those who were so soon to be left. They were just beginning to be conscious of their feebleness. But there is nothing more striking in the whole of the incidents of those forty days than the prominence which is given in them to the work of the Church when the Master had left it—and to the imperative obligations devolving upon it. And so here, not *encouragement*, but *obligation* is the inference that is drawn from that tremendous claim. "Because I have all power," Jesus in effect was saying, "therefore, you are charged with the duty of winning the world for its King." The all-ruling Christ calls for the universal proclamation of His sovereignty by His disciples. These five hundred early disciples little understood the sweep of the commandment. As history shows, they failed terribly to comprehend the emancipating power of it. But He says to us, as to them, "I am not content with the authority given to Me by God, unless I have the authority that each man for himself can give Me, by willing surrender of his heart and will to Me."

Jesus Christ craves no empty rule, no mere elevation by virtue of Divine supremacy, over men. He regards that elevation as incomplete without the voluntary surrender of men to become His disciples and champions, else He does not count that His universal power is established in a human heart. That dominion may be all-embracing like the ocean, and stretching into all corners of the universe, and dominating over all ages. Yet in that ocean there may stand up black and dry rocks, barren as they are dry, and blasted as they are black, because, with the awful power of a human will, men have said, "We will not have this Man to reign over us" (Luke 19:14). It is willing subjects whom Christ seeks to make the Divine grant of authority a reality.

In that work He needs His servants. The gift of God notwithstanding, the power of His cross notwithstanding, the perfection and completeness of His great reconciling and redeeming work notwithstanding, all these are vain unless we, His servants, will take them up in our hands as our weapons. We must go forth on the warfare to which He has summoned us. This is the command laid upon us all: "Make disciples of all nations." Only so will the reality correspond to the initial and all-embracing grant.

I do not have time to deal at all adequately, or in anything but the most superficial fashion, with the remaining parts of this great commission. "Make disciples of all nations"—that is the first thing. Then comes the second step: "Baptizing them in the name of the Father, and of the Son, and of the Holy Ghost" (Matt. 28:19).

Who are to be baptized? Now, notice, if I may venture to be slightly technical for a moment, that the word "nations" in the preceding clause is a neuter one, and that the word for "them" in this clause is a masculine, which seems to me fairly to imply that the command "baptizing them" does not refer to "all nations," but to the disciples latent among them, and to be drawn from them. Surely, surely, the great claim of absolute and unbounded power has for its consequence something better than the lame and impotent conclusion of appointing an indiscriminate rite as the means of making the disciples! Surely that is not in accordance with the spirituality of the Christian faith!

"Baptizing them in the name"—the name is one, that of the Father, and the Son, and the Holy Spirit. Does that mean the name of God, and of a man, and of an influence, all jumbled up together in blasphemous and irrational union? Surely, if Father, Son, and Holy Spirit have one name, the name of Divinity, then it is but a step to say that three Persons are one God!

But there is a great deal more here than a baptismal formula, for to be baptized into the Name is but the symbol of being plunged into the communion of this one threefold God of our salvation. The ideal state of the Christian disciple is that he shall be as a vase dropped into the Atlantic, encompassed about with God, and filled with Him. We all live, and move, and have our being in Him. But some of us have so wrapped ourselves, if I may venture to use such a figure, in waterproof covering, that, though we are floating in an ocean of Divinity, not a drop finds its way in! Cast it aside, and you will be saturated with God, and only in the measure in which you live and move and have your being in the Name are you disciples.

There is another step still. Making disciples and then bringing them into the communion with the Godhead is not all that is to flow from, and correspond to, and be realized in the individual. Also must come the absolute authority of Jesus Christ: "Teaching them to observe all things whatsoever I have commanded you."

We hear a great deal in these days about the worthlessness of mere dogmatic Christianity. Jesus Christ anticipated all that talk, and guarded it from exaggeration. For what He calls us here to train ourselves and others in, is not *creed* but *conduct*; not things to be believed—*credenda*—but things to be done—*agenda*—"teaching them to observe all things whatsoever I have commanded you" (Matt. 28:20). A creed that is not carried out in actions is empty; conduct that is not informed, penetrated, regulated by creed, is unworthy of a man, not to say of a Christian. What we are to *know* we are to know in order that we may *do*, and so inherit the benediction, which is never bestowed upon those who know, but upon those who, knowing these things, are blessed *in*, as well as *for*, the doing of them.

That training is to be continuous, educating to new views of duty; new applications of old truths, new sensitivity of conscience unveiling to us, ever as we climb, new heights to which we may aspire. The Christian Church has not yet learned—thank God it *is* learning, though by slow degrees—all the moral and practical implications and applications of "the truth as it is in Jesus." And so these are the three things by which the Church recognizes and corresponds to the universal dominion of Christ: making disciples universally; bringing them into the communion of the Father, the Son, and the Holy Spirit; and training them to conduct ever approximating more and more to the Divine ideal of humanity in the glorified Christ.

And now I must gather just into a sentence or two what is to be said about the last point. There is—

THE GREAT PROMISE

"I am with you alway, even unto the end of the world" (Matt. 28:20), or, as it might be read, "with you all the days, even to the accomplishment of the age." Note that emphatic "I am," which does not only denote certainty, but is the speech of Him who is lifted above the lower regions where time rolls and the succession of events occurs. That "I am" covers all the varieties of *was, is, will be.* Notice the long vista of variously tinted days which opens here: No matter how many they be, no matter how different their complexion, days of summer and days of winter, days of sunshine and days of storm, days of buoyant youth and days of stagnant, stereotyped old age, days of apparent failure and days of apparent prosperity, *He is with us in them all. They* change, but He is *"the same yesterday, and today, and forever"* (Heb. 13:8).

Notice the illimitable extent of the promise—"even unto the end." We are always tempted to think that long ago the earth was more full of God than it is today, and that away forward in the future it will again be fuller, but that this moment is comparatively empty. It seems the heavens touch the earth on the horizon in front and behind, and they are furthest above us just where we stand. But no past day had more of Christ in it than today has, and that He has gone away is the condition of His coming. He, therefore, departed for a season, that we might receive Him forever.

But note that the promise comes after a command, and is contingent, for all its blessedness and power, upon our obedience to the prescribed duty. That duty is primarily to make disciples of all nations, and the discharge of it is so closely connected with the realization of the promise that a non-missionary Church never has much of Christ's presence.

But obedience to all the King's commands is required if we are to stand before Him and enjoy His smile. If you wish to keep Christ very near you, and to feel Him with you, the way to do it is no mere cultivation of religious emotion, or saturating your mind with religious books and thoughts, though these have their place; but on the dusty road of life we must do His will and keep His commandments. "If a man love Me, he will keep My words: and My Father will love him, and We will come to him, and make Our abode with him" (John 14:23).

It is the ascended Christ who sends the Spirit upon men; it is the ascended Christ who opens men's hearts to hear; it is the ascended Christ who sends forth His messengers to the Gentiles; it is the ascended Christ who, today, is the energy of all the Church's power, the whiteness of all the Church's purity, the vitality of all the Church's life. He lives, and therefore, there is a Christian community on the face of the earth. He lives, and therefore, it will never die.

11

The Ascension

And He led them out as far as to Bethany, and He lifted up His hands, and blessed them. And it came to pass, while He blessed them, He was parted from them, and carried up into heaven.
—Luke 24:50,51

And when He had spoken these things, while they beheld, He was taken up; and a cloud received Him out of their sight. —Acts 1:9

Two of the four evangelists, Matthew and John, give no record of the Ascension. But the argument which infers ignorance from silence, which is always rash, is entirely discredited in this case. It is impossible to believe that Matthew, who wrote as the last word of his Gospel the great words, "All power is given unto Me in heaven and in earth. . . . lo! I am with you alway . . ." (28:18, 20), was ignorant of the fact which alone made these words credible. And it is equally impossible to believe that the evangelist who recorded the tender saying to Mary, "Go to My brethren, and say unto them, I ascend to My Father, and your Father" (John 20:17), was ignorant of its fulfillment.

The explanation of the silence is to be sought in a quite different direction. It comes from the fact that to the evangelists, rightly, the Ascension was but the prolongation and the culmination of the Resurrection. That being recorded, there was no need for the definite record of this.

There is another singular point about these records: Luke has two accounts, one in the end of his gospel, one in the beginning of Acts; and these two accounts are obviously different. The differences have been used by critics as a weapon with which to attack the veracity of both accounts. But there again a little consideration clears the path. The very places in which they respectively occur might have solved the difficulty, for the one is at the end of a book, and the other is at the beginning of a book; and so, naturally, the one regards the Ascension as the end of the earthly life, and the other as the beginning of the heavenly. The one is all suffused with evening light; the other is radiant with the promise of a new day. The one is the record of a tender farewell. In the other the sense of parting has almost been absorbed in the forward look to the new phase of relationship which is to begin.

If Luke had been a secular biographer, the critics would have been full of admiration at the delicacy of his touch, and the fineness of keeping in the two narratives, the picture being the same in both, and the scheme of coloring being different. But as he is only an evangelist, they criticize him for his "discrepancies." It is worth our while to take both his points of view.

But there is another thing to be remembered, that, as the appendix of his account of the Ascension in the book of the Acts, Luke tells us of the angel's message—"This same Jesus . . . shall so come in like manner" (Acts 1:11). So there are three points of view which have to be combined to get the whole significance of that mighty fact: the Ascension as an end; the Ascension as a beginning; the Ascension as the pledge of the return. Now take these three points.

First, we have the aspect of:

THE ASCENSION AS AN END

The narrative in Luke's gospel, in its very brevity, does yet distinctly suggest that retrospective and valedictory tone. Note how, for instance, we are told the locality—"He led them out as far as Bethany." The name at once strikes a chord of remembrance. What memories clustered around it, and how natural it was that the parting should take place there, not merely because the crest of the Mount of Olives hid the place from the gaze of the crowded city; but because it was within earshot almost of the home where so much of the sweet earthly fellowship (that was now to end) had passed!

The same note of regarding the scene as being the termination of those blessed years of dear and familiar fellowship is struck in the fact, so human, so natural, that He lifted His hands to bless them, moved by the same impulse with which so often we have wrung a hand at parting, and stammered, "God bless you!" And the same valedictory hue is further deepened by the fact that what Luke puts first is not the Ascension, but the parting. "He was parted from them," that is the main fact; "and He was carried up into heaven," comes almost as a subordinate one. At all events it is regarded mainly as being the medium by which the parting was effected.

So the aspect of the Ascension thus presented is that of a tender farewell—the pathetic conclusion of three long, blessed years. And yet that is not all, for the evangelist adds a very enigmatic word: "(They) returned to Jerusalem with great joy" (Luke 24:52). Glad because He had gone? No. Glad merely because He had gone up? No. The saying is a riddle, left at the end of the book, for readers to ponder, and it is a subtle link with what is to be written in the next volume, when the aspect of the Ascension as an end is subordinate, and its aspect as a beginning is prominent. So regarded, it filled the disciples with joy.

Thus you see, I think, that without any illegitimate straining of the expressions of the text, we do come to the point of view from which, to begin with, this great event must be looked at. We have to take the same view, and to regard that Ascension not only as the end of an epoch of sweet friendship, but as the solemn close and culmination of the whole earthly life. I have no time to dwell upon the thoughts that come crowding into one's mind when we take that point of view. But let me suggest, in the briefest way, one or two of them.

Here is an end which circles around to, and is of a piece with, the beginning. "I came forth from the Father, and am come into the world: again, I leave the world, and go unto the Father" (John 16:28). The Ascension corresponds with (and meets the miracle of) the Incarnation. And as the Word who became flesh, came by the natural path of human birth, and entered in through the gate by which we all enter, and yet came as none else have come, by His own will, in the miracle of His Incarnation, so at the end He passed out from life through the gate by which we all pass, and "was obedient unto death, even the death of the cross." And yet He passed likewise on a path which none but Himself have trod, and ascended up to heaven, whence He had descended to earth. He came into the world, not as leaving the Father, for He is "the Son of Man which is in heaven" (John 3:13), for He is with us "alway, even to the end of the world" (Matt. 28:20). Thus the Incarnation and the Ascension support each other.

But let me remind you how, in this connection, we have the very same combination of lowliness and gentleness with majesty and power which runs through the whole of the story of the earthly life of Jesus Christ. He was born in a stable, and waited on by angels, the subject of all the humiliations of humanity, and flashing forth through them all the power of Divinity. He ascends on high at last, and yet with no pomp nor visible splendor to the world, but only in the presence of a handful of loving hearts, choosing some dimple of the hill where its folds hid them from the city.

As quietly and silently as He came into the world, so quietly and silently He passed from it. In this connection there is more than the picturesque contrast between the rapture of Elijah, with its whirlwind, and chariot of fire and horses of fire, and the calm, slow rising, by no external medium raised, of the Christ. It was fitting that the mortal should be swept up into the unfamiliar heaven by the pomp of angels and the chariot of fire. It was fitting that when Jesus ascended to His "own calm home, His habitation from eternity," there should be nothing visible but His own slowly rising form, with hands uplifted, to shed benediction on the heads of those who gazed from beneath.

In like manner, regarding the Ascension as an end, may we not say that it is the seal of heaven impressed on the sacrifice of the cross? "Wherefore God also hath highly exalted Him, and given Him a Name which is above every name; that at the Name of Jesus every knee should bow" (Phil. 2:9,10). We find in that intimate connection between the cross and the Ascension, the key to the deep saying which carries references to both in itself, when the Lord spoke of Himself as being lifted up and drawing all men unto Him. The original primary reference no doubt was to this elevation on the cross, "as Moses lifted up the serpent" (John 3:14). But the final, and at the time of its being spoken, the mysterious, reference was to the fact that in descending to the depth of humiliation He was rising to the height of glory.

The zenith of the Ascension is the rebound from the nadir of the cross. The lowliness of the stoop measures the loftiness of the elevation, and the Son of Man was most profoundly abased. The cross and the Ascension, if I might use so violent a figure, are like the twin stars, of which the heavens present some examples, one dark and lusterless, one flashing with radiancy of light, but knit together by an invisible bond, and revolving around a common center. When He "parted from them, and was carried up into heaven," He ended the humiliation which caused the elevation.

And then, again, I might suggest that, regarded in its aspect as an end, this Ascension is also the culmination and the natural conclusion of the Resurrection. As I have said, the Scripture point of view with reference to these two is not that they are two, but that the one is the starting-point of the line of which the other is the goal. The process which began when He rose from the dead, whatever view we may take of the condition of His earthly life during the forty days of parenthesis, could have no ending, rational and intelligible, except the Ascension. Thus we should think of it not only as the end of a sweet friendship, but as the end of the gracious manifestation of the earthly life, the counterpart of the Incarnation and descent to earth, the end of the cross and the culmination of the Resurrection. The Son of Man, the same who also descended into the lowest parts of the earth, ascended up where He was before.

Now let us turn to the other aspect which the evangelist gives, when He ceases to be an evangelist, and becomes a church historian. *Then* he considers:

THE ASCENSION AS A BEGINNING

The place which it holds in the Acts of the Apostles explains the point of view from which the Ascension is to be regarded. It is the foundation of everything that the writer has afterwards to say. It is the basis of the Church. It is the ground of all the activity which Christ's servants put forth. Not only its place explains this aspect of it, but the very first words of the book itself do the same: "The former treatise have I made . . . of all that Jesus began both to do and teach" (Acts 1:1)—and now I am to tell you of an Ascension, and of all that Jesus continued to do and teach, says Luke. So that the Acts is the history of the work of the Lord, who was able to do that work, just because He had ascended up on high.

The same impression is produced if we ponder the conversation which precedes the account of the Ascension in the book of Acts. Though it touches the same topics as are touched by the words that precede the account in the gospel, yet it presents them in a different aspect. It suggests the endowments with which the Christian community is to be invested, and the work which therefore it is to do, because of the Ascension of Jesus Christ. The apostle Peter had caught that thought when, on the day of Pentecost, he said, "Therefore being by the right hand of God exalted . . . He hath shed forth this, which ye now see and hear" (Acts 2:33). And throughout the whole book the same point of view is kept up. "The work that is done upon earth He doeth it all Himself."

So there is in *this* narrative nothing about parting, there is nothing about blessing. There is simply the ascending up, and the significant addition of the reception into the cloud, which, while He was yet plainly visible, and not dwindled by distance into a speck, received Him out of their sight. The cloud was the symbol of the Divine Presence. It had hung over the Tabernacle, which had sat between the cherubim, which had wrapped the shepherds and the angels on the hillside. It shown down in its brightness on the Mount of Transfiguration, and now, as the symbol of the Divine Presence, it received the ascending Lord. It showed the men who stood gazing up into heaven, that He had passed to the right hand of the Majesty on high.

Thus we have to think of that Ascension as being the groundwork and foundation of all the world-wide and age-long energy which the living Christ is exercising today. As one of the other evangelists, or, at least, the appendix to his Gospel, puts it, He ascended up on high, and "they went forth, and preached everywhere, the Lord working with them, and confirming the word with signs following" (Mark 16:20).

It is the ascended Christ who sends the Spirit upon men; it is the ascended Christ who opens men's hearts to hear; it is the ascended Christ who sends forth His messengers to the Gentiles; it is the ascended Christ who, today, is the energy of all the Church's power, the whiteness of all the Church's purity, the vitality of all the Church's life. He lives, and therefore, there is a Christian community on the face of the earth. He lives, and therefore, it will never die.

So we, too, have to look to that risen Lord as being the power by which alone any of us can do either great or small work in

His Church. That Ascension is symbolically put as being to "the right hand of God." What is the right hand of God? The Divine omnipotence. Where is it? Everywhere. What does sitting at the right hand of God mean? Wielding the powers of omnipotence. And so He says, "All power is given unto Me"; and He is doing a work today, wider in its aspects than (though it be the application and consequence of) the work upon the cross. He cried here, "It is finished!" (John 19:30), but "the work of the ascended Jesus" will never be finished until "the kingdoms of this world are become the kingdoms of our Lord, and of His Christ" (Rev. 11:15).

There are other aspects of His work in heaven which space will not allow me to dwell upon, though I cannot but summarize them briefly here. By the Ascension Christ begins to prepare a place for us. How could any of us stand in the presence of that eternal Light if He were not there? We should be like some savage or rustic swept up suddenly and put down in the middle of the glittering ring of courtiers around a throne, unless we could lift our eyes and recognize a known and loving face there. Where Christ is, I can be. He has taken one human nature up into the glory, and other human natures will therefore find that it is a home.

To use the symbolism which one of the New Testament writers employs for illustration of a thought far greater than the symbol, the ascended Christ, like a High Priest, has passed within the veil: "now to appear in the presence of God for us" (Heb. 9:24). And the intercession which is far more than petition, and is the whole action of that dear Lord who identifies us with Himself, and whose mighty work is ever present before the Divine mind as an element in His dealings, that intercession is being carried on forever for us all. So, "set your affections on things above" (Col. 3:2), where Christ is sitting at the right hand of God. Therefore, expect His help in your work, and do the work which He has left you to carry on here. So, face death and the dim kingdoms beyond, without quiver and without doubt, assured that where the treasure is, there the heart will be also; and that where the Master is, there the servants who follow in His steps will be also at last.

THE ASCENSION AS BEING
THE PLEDGE OF THE RETURN

The two men in white apparel who stood by gently rebuked the gazers for gazing into heaven. They would not have rebuked them for gazing, if they could have seen Him, but to look into the empty heaven was useless. And they added the reason why the heavens need not be looked at, as long as there is the earth to stand on: "This same Jesus, which is taken up from you into heaven, shall so come in like manner as ye have seen Him go" (Acts 1:11). Note the emphatic declaration of identity: "this *same* Jesus." Note the use of the simple human name: "this same *Jesus*," and recall the thoughts that cluster around it, of the ascended humanity, and the perpetual humanity of the ascended Lord, "the same yesterday, and today, and forever."

Note also the strong assertion of visible, corporeal return: "Shall *so* come in *like* manner as ye have seen Him go." That return is no metaphor, no mere piece of rhetoric. It is not to be eviscerated of its contents by being taken as a synonym for the diffusion of His influence all over a regenerated race. But it points to the return of the Man Jesus locally, corporeally, visibly. "We believe that Thou shalt come to be our Judge"; we believe that Thou wilt come to take Thy servants home.

The world has not seen the last of Jesus Christ. Such an Ascension, after such a life, cannot be the end of Him. "As it is appointed unto men once to die, but after death the judgment: So Christ was once offered to bear the sins of many . . . shall He appear the second time without sin unto salvation" (Heb. 9:27,28). As inevitably as for sinful human nature judgment follows death, so inevitably for the sinless Man, who is the sacrifice for the world's sins, His judicial return shall follow His atoning work. He will come again, having received the Kingdom, to take account with His servants, and to perfect their possession of the salvation which by His Incarnation, Passion, Resurrection, and Ascension, He wrought for the world.

Therefore, one sweet face and one great fact—the face of the Christ, the fact of the cross—should fill the past. One sweet face, one great fact—the face of the Christ, the fact of His presence with us all the days—should fill the present. One regal face, one great hope, should fill the future; the face of the King who sits upon the throne, the hope that He will come again, and "so we shall be ever with the Lord."

. . . a risen life is the type of all noble life, and before there can be a risen life there must have been a death. True, we may say that the spiritual facts in a man's experience, which are represented by these two great symbols of a death and a rising, are but like the segment of a circle which, seen from the one side is convex and from the other is concave. But however loosely we may feel that the metaphors represent the facts, this is plain, that unless man dies to flesh, to self-will, to the world, he never will live a life that is worth calling life.

12

Risen with Christ

If ye then be risen with Christ, seek those things which are above, where Christ sitteth on the right hand of God. Set your affection on things above, not on things on the earth. —Colossians 3:1-2

We have been considering the Resurrection and Ascension of Jesus Christ in a series of sermons, and in this one I wish to turn to the thought that *the followers of the risen Christ are risen.* There are three aspects in which the New Testament treats the Resurrection, and these three seem to have successively come into the consciousness of the Church.

First, as is natural, it was considered mainly in its bearing on the person and work of our Lord. We may take for illustration the way in which the Resurrection is treated in the earliest of the apostolic discourses, as recorded in the Acts of the Apostles.

Then it came, with further reflection and experience, to be discerned that it had a bearing on the hope of the immortality of man.

And last of all, as the Christian life deepened, it came to be discerned that the Resurrection was the pattern of the life of the Christian disciples.

It was regarded first as a witness, then as a prophecy, then as a symbol. Three fragments of Scripture express these three phrases: for the first, "Declared to be the Son of God with power . . . by the Resurrection from the dead" (Rom. 1:4); for the second, "Now is Christ risen from the dead, and become the firstfruits of them that slept" (1 Cor. 15:20); for the third, "(God) hath raised us up together, and made us sit together in heavenly places" (Eph. 2:6). I have considered incidentally the two former aspects in the course of previous chapters; I wish to turn at present to the final third one.

One more observation I must make by way of introduction, and that is, that the way in which the apostle here glides from "being risen with Christ" to "where Christ is, sitting at the right hand of God," confirms what I have pointed out in former discourses, that the Ascension of Jesus Christ is always considered in Scripture as being nothing more than the necessary outcome and issue of the process which began in the Resurrection. They are not separate facts, but they are two ends of one process. And so with these thoughts, that Resurrection develops into Ascension, and that in both Jesus Christ is the pattern for His followers, let us turn to the words before us.

First, we have here

THE CHRISTIAN LIFE CONSIDERED
AS A RISEN LIFE

We are all familiar with the great evangelical point of view from which the death and Resurrection of Jesus Christ are usually contemplated. To many of us Christ's sacrifice is nothing more or less than the means by which the world is reconciled to God, and Christ's Resurrection is nothing more than the seal which was set by Divinity upon that work. "(Crucified) for our offenses, and raised again for our justification" (Rom. 4:25), as Paul has it—that is the point of view from which most evangelical or orthodox

Christian people are contented to regard the solemn fact of the
death and the radiant fact of the Resurrection.

We cannot be too emphatic about these truths, but we may
be too exclusive in our contemplation of them. We do well
when we say that they are the gospel; we do not well when we
say, as some do, that they are the *whole* gospel. For there is
another stream of teaching in the New Testament, of which
my text is an example, and a multitude of other passages that I
cannot refer to now are equally conspicuous instances. In this
stream death and Resurrection are regarded, not so much in
respect to the power which they exercise in the reconciliation
of the world to God, as in their aspect as the type of all noble
and true Christian life. You remember how, when our Lord
Himself touched upon the fruitful issues of His death, and said:
"Except a corn of wheat fall into the ground an die, it abideth
alone: but if it die, it bringeth forth much fruit" (John 12:24),
He at once went on to say that a man who loved his life would
lose it. He added that a man who lost his life would find it, and
proceeded to point, even then, and in this connection, to His
cross as our pattern, declaring: "If any man serve Me, let him
follow Me; and where I am, there shall also My servant be"
(John 12:26).

> Made like Him, like Him we rise;
> Ours the cross, the grave, the skies.

So, then, a risen life is the type of all noble life, and before
there can be a risen life there must have been a death. True, we
may say that the spiritual facts in a man's experience, which are
represented by these two great symbols of a death and a rising,
are but like the segment of a circle which, seen from the one
side is convex and from the other is concave. But however
loosely we may feel that the metaphors represent the facts, this
is plain, that unless man dies to flesh, to self-will, to the world,
he never will live a life that is worth calling life.

The condition of all nobleness and all growth upwards is

that we shall die daily, and live a life that has sprung victorious from the death of self. All lofty ethics teach, and Christianity teaches it, with redoubled emphasis, because it says to us, that the cross and the Resurrection are not merely imaginative emblems of the noble and the Christian life. They are a great deal more than that. For do not forget—if you do, you will be hopelessly at sea as to large tracts of blessed Christian truth—that by faith in Jesus Christ we are brought into a true deep union with Him.

This is true in no mere metaphorical or analogous sense, but in most blessed reality. At conversion there comes into the believing heart a spark of the life that is Christ's own. With Him we do live, and from Him we do live a life cognate with His. He, having risen from the dead, dies no more, and over Him death has no dominion. So it is not a metaphor only, but a spiritual truth, when we speak of being risen with Christ. Our faith, in the measure of its genuineness, its depth and its operative power upon our characters, will be the gate through which there shall pass into our deadness the life that truly is. This life has nothing to do with death or sin. And this unity with Jesus, received by faith, results in the fact that the depths of the Christian life are hid with Christ in God. We, risen with Him, do even now sit "at the right hand in heavenly places." At the same time our feet, dusty and sometimes blood-stained, are journeying along the paths of life.

This is the great teaching of my text, and of a multitude of other places; and this is the teaching which modern Christianity, in its exclusive, or all but exclusive, contemplation of the cross as the sacrifice for sin, has far too much forgotten. "Ye are risen with Christ."

This veritable death and rising again, which marks the Christian life, is set forth before us in the initial baptismal rite of the Christian Church. Some do not agree with me in my view, either of what is the mode or of who are the subjects of that ordinance, but if you know anything about the question, you know that everyone who has a right to give a judgment agrees

with us Baptists in saying—although they must not think that it
carries anything obligatory upon the practice of today—that the
primitive Church baptized by immersion. Now, the meaning of
baptism is to symbolize these two inseparable moments, dying to
sin, to self, to the world, to the old past, and rising again to
newness of life. Our sacramentarian friends say that, in my text,
it was in baptism that these Colossian Christians rose again with
Christ. I, for my part, do not believe that. I believe that their
baptism was the outward sign of what lies at the gate of a true
Christian life. Of that I have no doubt.

So the first thought of our text is not only taught in words,
but it stands manifest in the ritual of the Church as it was from
the beginning. We die, and we rise again, through faith and by
union through faith, with Christ "that died, yea rather, that is
risen again, who is even at the right hand of God" (Rom. 8:34).

Let me turn, secondly, to

THE CONSEQUENT AIMS
OF THE CHRISTIAN LIFE

"If ye then be risen with Christ, seek those things which are
above" (Col. 3:1). "To seek" implies the direction of the external life toward certain objects. It is not to seek as if perhaps we
might not find; it is not even to seek in the sense of searching
for, but it is to seek in the sense of aiming at. And now do you
not think that if we had burning in our hearts, and felt in our
experience, the sense of union with Jesus Christ the risen Savior, that would shape the direction and dictate the aims of our
earthly life? As surely as the elevation of the rocket tube deter-
mines the flight of the projectile that comes from it, so surely
would the inward consciousness (if it were vivid as it ought to be
in all Christian people) of that risen life throbbing within the
heart, shape all the external conduct. It would give us wings and
make us soar. It would make us buoyant, and lift us above the
creeping aims that constitute the objects of life for so many
men.

But you say, "Things above: that is an indefinite phrase. What do you mean by it?" I will tell you what the Bible means by it. It means Jesus Christ. All the nebulous splendors of that firmament are gathered together in one blazing sun. It is a vague direction to tell man to shoot up, into an empty heaven. It is not a vague direction to tell him to seek the "things above"; for they are all gathered into a person. "Where Christ is, sitting at the right hand of God"—that is the meaning of "things above," which are to be the continual aim of the man who is conscious of a risen life. And, of course, they will be. If we feel, as we ought to feel habitually, though with varying clearness, that we do carry within us a spark, if I might use that phrase, of the very life of Jesus Christ, so surely as fire will spring upward, so surely as water will rise to the height of its source, so surely will our outward lives be directed toward Him. He is the life of our inward lives, and the goal, therefore, of our outward actions.

Jesus Christ is the summing up of "the things that are above"; therefore, one great truth stands out clearly. The only aim for a Christian soul, consistent with the facts of its Christian life, is to be *like* Christ, to be *with* Christ, to *please* Christ.

How does that aim—"Wherefore we labor, that, whether present or absent, we may be well accepted of Him" (2 Cor. 5:9)—how does that aim bear upon the multitude of inferior and nearer aims which men pursue, and which Christians have to pursue along with other men? How does it bear upon them? In this way: As the culminating peak of a mountain-chain bears on the lower hills that for miles and miles buttress it, and hold it up, and aspire toward it, and find their perfection in its calm summit that touches the skies.

The more we have in view, as our aim in life, Christ who is "at the right hand of God," and assimilation, communion with Him, approbation from Him, the more will all immediate aims be ennobled, and delivered from the evils that otherwise cleave to them. They are more when they are second than when they are first. "Seek ye first the Kingdom of God" (Matt. 6:33), and all your other aims—as students, as thinkers, as scientists, as men of business, as parents, as lovers, or anything else—will be enlarged by being subordinated to the conscious aim of pleasing Him. That aim should persist, like a strain of melody, one long, held-down, diapason note, through all our lives. Perfume can be diffused into the air, and dislodge no atom of that which it makes fragrant. This supreme aim can be pursued through, and by means of, all nearer ones, and is inconsistent with nothing but sin. "Seek the things that are above."

Lastly, we have here—

THE DISCIPLINE NEEDED TO SECURE THE RIGHT DIRECTION OF THE LIFE

The apostle does not content himself with pointing out the aims. He adds practical advice as to how these aims can be made dominant in our individual cases, when he says, "Set your affections on things above." "Affections" is not the full sense of the word that is here employed, and the Revised Version gives a more adequate rendering when it says, "Set your *minds* on the things that are above." A man cannot do with his love according to his will. He cannot say: "*Resolved*, that I love So-and-so"; and then set himself to do it. But though you cannot act on the emotions directly by the will, you *can* act directly on your understandings, on your thoughts, and your thoughts will act on your affections.

If a man wants to love Jesus Christ he must think about Him. That is plain English. It is vain for a man to try to coerce his wandering affections by any other course than by concentrating his thoughts. Set your minds on the things that are above, and that will consolidate and direct your emotions; and the thoughts and the emotions together will shape the outward efforts. Seeking the things that are above will come, and will only come, when mind and heart and inward life are occupied with Him.

There is no other way by which the externals can be made right than by setting a watch on the door of our hearts and minds, and this inward discipline must be put in force before there will be any continuity or sureness in the outward aim. For that direction of the life of which I have been speaking, we need a clear perception and a concentrated purpose, and we shall not get either of these unless we fall back, by thought and meditation, upon the truths which will provide them both.

There is another aspect concerning the connection between these two parts of our text. Not only is setting our thoughts on the things above the way by which we can make these the aim of our lives. They are not only *aims* to be reached at some future stage of our progress, but they are *possessions* to be enjoyed at the present. We may have a present Christ and a present heaven. The Christian life is not all aspiration; it is fruition as well. We have to seek, but even as we seek, we should be conscious that we possess what we are seeking—even while we seek it! Do you know anything of that double experience of having the things that are above, here and now, as well as reaching out toward them?

I am afraid that the Christian life of this generation suffers at a thousand points. It seems to be more concerned with the ordering of the outward life, and the manifold activities which this busy generation has struck out for itself, than it is with the quiet setting of the mind on the things that are above. Oh, if we would think more about things above we should aim more at them; and if we were sure that we possessed them today we should be more eager for a larger possession tomorrow!

We may all gain that risen life for our own, if we will knit ourselves, in humble dependence and utter self-surrender, to the Christ who died for us that we might rise to righteousness. And if we have Him, in any deep and real sense, as the life of our lives, then we will be blessed, amid all the divergent and sometimes conflicting nearer aims which we have to pursue. Then we will see clearly above them that to which they all may tend: the one aim which corresponds to a man's nature, which meets his condition, which satisfies his needs, which can always be attained if it is followed, and which when secured never disappoints.

God help us all to say with Paul, "This one thing I do, and all else I count but dung, that I may know Him, and the power of His Resurrection, and the fellowship of His sufferings, being made conformable unto His death, if by any means I may attain unto the Resurrection from the dead!" This should be our "after the Resurrection" prayer!

Study Guide

CHAPTER ONE

The Grave of the Dead John and the Grave of the Living Jesus

1. How would you compare and contrast the two "schools" discussed in this chapter—those of John the Baptist and Jesus?
2. Can you think of other "schools" that died after their founder's death?
3. Can you think of other "schools" that *continued* after their founder's death?
4. How would you answer the questions raised on page 15:

   - What had lifted them suddenly so far above themselves? Their Master's death?

   - Why, then, do they thus strangely blaze up into grandeur and heroism?

   - Can any reasonable account be given of these paradoxes?

   - Why did they not do as John's disciples did, and disappear?

   - Why was not the stream lost in the sand, when the headwaters were cut off?

5. React to the statement at the top of page 17: "And it is important to observe that, even if we had not the documentary evidence of the Pauline epistles as the earliest records of the gospels, and of the Acts of the Apostles, we should still have sufficient proof that the belief in the resurrection is as old as the church."

6. Reread the author's discussion of "hallucinations" on page 19. Is this theory still propounded by critics of Christianity today?

7. How do you feel when you read "then he is not gone from us altogether"?

8. On page 21 the author says: "The power of Christ's resurrection as the pattern and pledge of ours is the final source of the joy which may fill our hearts as we turn away from that empty sepulcher." Has this been your experience?

CHAPTER TWO

Touch Me Not

1. React to the author's statement on page 27: "The two apostles ran to the tomb. She seems to have come, not with them, but after them. Manlike, they satisfied themselves of the fact and went away. Womanlike, she hung about the place unable to tear herself from it, and yet, since the grave was empty, having no reason for staying." Do you agree that the reactions detailed here are typically masculine and feminine?

2. Do you agree that her "grief was beginning to be selfish"? Or was this simply a progressive realization of her loss? Why do you suppose Mary did not at the first recognize the risen Lord?

3. Why and what was the touch that was forbidden?

4. Discuss the ramifications of the statement on page 31: "If, then, we would rightly understand what that ascension to the Father means, we must see the teaching implied here. We must recognize that it is a step toward, not the absence of the Lord *from* His people, but the continual presence of the Lord *with* His people."

5. MacLaren says: "We can sit with Him in the heavenly places, and He comes and works with us in the earthly places." What does this dichotomy mean to you? In what senses are the two sides of this sweeping statement true in your life?

CHAPTER THREE

The Denier Alone with His Lord

1. MacLaren describes Peter's experience as one of " . . . a melted heart, true penitence, and profound sorrow." How does this compare to the typical steps in the conversion experience?
2. What does the author's exposition of Peter's personality tell you about that apostle? Do you agree with MacLaren's conclusion: "For a continuous life in contradiction to our profession is a blacker crime than a momentary fall. They who 'year in and year out,' call themselves Christians, and deny their profession by the whole tenor of their lives, are more deeply guilty than was the apostle."
3. Is the statement at the bottom of page 39 a comfort to you—or a condemnation: "But Jesus Christ comes to us, and no sin of ours, no denial of ours, can bar His lingering, His reproachful, and yet His restoring, love and grace"?
4. Compare Peter's experience with the risen Savior to the prodigal son's reception by his father. Any similarities? Any differences?
5. How did you answer the question on page 41: "Do you not think that when the apostle saw in Christ's face, and heard from His lips, the full assurance of forgiveness, he was far more ashamed of himself than he had ever been in the hours of bitterest remorse?" How can a parent apply this insight? A child?
6. "*The consciousness of forgiveness* may be gradual; *the fact of forgiveness* is instantaneous" (p. 42). Discuss the ramifications of this statement.
7. MacLaren discourses at some length about the value of one's being "alone" with the Savior. Contemplate your own experience. What did you learn when you were thus alone?

CHAPTER FOUR

The Travelers to Emmaus

1. On page 49 MacLaren says, " . . . a seeking *mind* is as sure to find God as a seeking *heart*." What does he mean by this? Which "way" did you come to the Lord?
2. Look up the article on "Cleopas" in a Bible dictionary or

encyclopedia. What insight does this episode in Emmaus give you into the post-resurrection ministry of Jesus? Does it help you to compare His earthly ministry to His heavenly ministry?

3. On page 51 MacLaren says: " . . . the risen Lord joyfully companies with the humblest seeker after light." What does this truth mean to you?

4. MacLaren says the two Emmaus disciples " . . . were lamenting not the departure of a beloved Friend, but the fall of a Leader; and with the fall of a Leader, the loss of a cause." Do you think that was true of the other better-known disciples as well?

5. The meaning of the death of Jesus was misunderstood at the time of His crucifixion, and also today. What is the difference with the misunderstandings of people today?

6. MacLaren says that Jesus *does not abide with us uninvited.* What does he mean by that?

7. He also says, "They who know the risen Christ do not need His bodily presence." What does that statement mean to you? Do you agree with it?

CHAPTER FIVE

The Risen Lord's Charge and Gift

1. MacLaren says that "officialism is the dry-rot of all churches. . . ." Do you agree? If so, why? If not, why? What do you think he means by "officialism"? What are some other names for it?

2. On page 63 MacLaren says: "We are the representatives of Jesus Christ, and if I might dare to use such a phrase, He is to be incarnated again in the hearts, and manifested again in the lives, of His servants." Are we to be "reflectors" of His light? Is this what Jesus meant when He said we are "the light of the world"?

3. On page 65 the author says: " . . . it is because the Christian Church as a whole, and we as individual members of it, so imperfectly realize the ABC of our faith, our absolute dependence on the inbreathed life of Jesus Christ, that so much of our work is merely ploughing the sands. So often we labor in vain and spend our strength for nothing." This is a shattering indictment of the church. Do you agree with it? Do you see any signs of improvement in the church today?

4. He also says that sometimes "ice plugs the service-pipe." What plugs can you think of that plague the modern-day church? What problems did they have in the early church? (Discuss people like Ananias and Sapphira.)

5. On page 66 MacLaren quotes the old saying, "the same heat softens wax and hardens clay." What does this mean to you? Can you think of any examples?

CHAPTER SIX

Thomas and Jesus

1. Do you agree with MacLaren's assessment of Thomas as guilty of "dogged disbelief" and "arrogant assumption"? Read the article on Thomas in a Bible encyclopedia or dictionary and compare it to MacLaren's development of the character of the "stiff unbeliever" (see p. 71).

2. Like Peter, Thomas seems to have been a blending of bravery and brashness, courage and cowardice. Compare these two disciples and list their strengths and weaknesses.

3. MacLaren seems to think Thomas' predominant personality trait was to be "melancholy." Do you agree? How would you characterize Peter?

4. Do you feel "isolation" was Thomas' problem?

5. Do you agree that Thomas was a "disbeliever" rather than a "doubter"?

6. On page 78 MacLaren says: "Christian faith, being more than intellectual belief, does involve the activity of the will. Credence is the starting-point, but it is no more than that. There may be belief in the truth of the gospel and not a spark of faith in the Christ revealed by the gospel." On page 79 he says: "Faith is . . . the sight of the inward eye. . . . the direct perception of the unseen." Come up with your own definitions of faith and apply them to your own life. Do you agree with what MacLaren says here?

CHAPTER SEVEN

The Sea and the Beach

1. Compare the first appearance of Jesus recorded in Matthew 4 and Mark 1 with this post-resurrection appearance. What are the similarities? The differences?
2. What happened to the disciples as a result of the two experiences?
3. Shepherds were the first to worship the Infant Jesus, and "toiling fishermen" were prominent among His followers after His resurrection. Compare the two occupations. Why do you suppose Jesus so strongly appealed to and attracted "outdoorsmen" such as these?
4. What does it mean to you that Jesus is interested in your occupation?
5. On page 87 MacLaren says: "The eye that sees the Lord amidst the whirl of earthly things, sees all that it needs for peace and power." Put this thought in your own words and also contemplate the various facets of meaning it contains.
6. Contrast the reactions of impetuous Peter and contemplative John to this appearance of Jesus. How do you think you would have responded to this exciting event?
7. Compare and contrast the two meals: "the Lord's Supper" and "the supper on the shore." What were the similarities? The differences?

CHAPTER EIGHT

Lovest Thou Me?

1. Why do you think Jesus singled out Peter in this post-resurrection episode?
2. On page 96 MacLaren says: " . . . there can be no better discipline for us all than to remember our faults. As we remember the awfulness of our sins, we can rejoice that God in Christ has forgotten them. The beginning of Christ's merciful treatment of the forgiven Peter is to compel him to remember, that he may learn and be ashamed." Peter had to learn many lessons in his walk with the Lord. Which lesson do you think made the biggest impression on him?

3. Compare "filial" or brotherly love in your mind to the kind of sacrificial love Jesus is calling for here. What do you think has to happen in our lives as believers to bring us to this advanced stage of discipleship?

4. On page 99 MacLaren says: "Any sin is inconsistent with Christian love to Christ. Thank God we have no right to say of any sin that it is incompatible with this love! More than that; a great, gross, flagrant, sudden fall like Peter's is a great deal less inconsistent with love to Christ than are the continuously unworthy, worldly, selfish, Christ-forgetting lives of hosts of complacent, professing Christians today." Do you agree with his assessment?

5. What is implied in the author's statement on page 100: "We need the profession of words; we need, as Peter himself enjoined at a subsequent time, to be ready to 'give an answer to every man that asketh you a reason of the hope' (1 Peter 3:15), and an acknowledgment of the love, that are in us. But if you want others to believe in your love, however Jesus Christ may know it, go and work in the Master's vineyard"? How does this square with the conclusion of James: "Faith without works is dead"?

6. How would you describe your life of faith today? A year ago?

CHAPTER NINE

Doing and Staying

1. MacLaren says, "Jesus calls for no recruits under false pretenses" (p. 105). How does this compare with some of the Bible teachers or teachings currently being dispensed?

2. The author says: "He died for you and me first, before He asked us to be ready to die for Him. . . . Only the risen Lord . . . has the right to bid us die for Him." (p. 106). Do you agree? Why or why not?

3. Suffering sometimes follows surrender for the Christian, says MacLaren. What has been your experience in this regard? What are the various forms that "suffering for Christ" can take? Can you think of examples in your own family or among your acquaintances?

4. On page 106 MacLaren says: "No noble life is possible unless it be a sacrificial life." What does he mean by this?
5. Read General Booth's testimony on pages 108 and 109 and J. Wilbur Chapman's assessment "that the greatness of a man's power is the measure of his surrender." What is he saying? Do you agree?
6. "The life of service and the life of waiting" are the double manifestations of the Christian life. Have you found this to be true?

CHAPTER TEN

On the Mountain

1. From whom do you think Paul learned about the appearance of Jesus to "five hundred brethren at once" recorded in 1 Corinthians 15:6?
2. On page 119 MacLaren says: "No system (Christianity) so condemns human nature as it is; none thinks so glowingly of human nature as it may become." Think about and discuss the ramifications of this statement.
3. Reread the author's discussion of the Great Commission. Where do you see yourself fitting into this picture? Your church? Your business (occupation)?
4. On page 122 MacLaren says: " . . . what He calls us here to train ourselves and others in, is not *creed* but *conduct*; not things to be believed—*credenda*—but things to be done—*agenda*—'teaching them to observe all things whatsoever I have commanded you' (Matt. 28:20). A creed that is not carried out in actions is empty; conduct that is not informed, penetrated, regulated by creed, is unworthy of a man, not to say of a Christian. What we are to *know* we are to know in order that we may *do*." Think about this in the light of what the apostle James taught in his epistle. Does he agree—or disagree—with MacLaren?
5. Reread what MacLaren says in the second paragraph on page 123. Do you agree with him?

CHAPTER ELEVEN

The Ascension

1. On page 128 the author says: "If Luke had been a secular biographer, the critics would have been full of admiration at the

delicacy of his touch, and the fineness of keeping in the two narratives, the picture being the same in both, and the scheme of coloring being different." Do you agree with his assessment? What would be different about a secular biography of Jesus?

2. MacLaren sees that Luke is both an evangelist (in the Gospel of Luke) and a church historian (in Acts). Do you agree? Is there a difference?

3. What difference would it have made in the history of the early church if the Gospel had been proclaimed through the existing religious hierarchy?

4. Reread the paragraph on page 134 describing what heaven would be like if Jesus hadn't gone before us. Do you agree with the author's description?

5. "The world has not seen the last of Jesus Christ" (p. 135). What difference should this make in our lives?

CHAPTER TWELVE

Risen with Christ

1. "As the Christian life deepened (in those early Christians), it came to be discerned that the Resurrection was the pattern of the life of the Christian disciples. It was discerned first as a *witness*, then as a *prophecy*, then as a *symbol*" (pp. 139-140). Think about and discuss those three perceptions.

2. Reread the excerpt at the beginning of the chapter (see also p. 41). Think about and discuss the author's metaphor of the Christian life.

3. What does it mean to "die daily"?

4. How is the Christian life like baptism?

5. Discuss how "things above " means Jesus Christ. Explore the ramifications of this truth.

6. "Things above" is also referred to as "possessions." How is this true?

7. On page 146 MacLaren says: "We may all gain that risen life for our own, if we will knit ourselves, in humble dependence and utter self-surrender, to the Christ who died for us that we might rise to righteousness." Is this a reachable goal or is it an oversimplification?